Exotic Pets
A Veterinary Guide for Owners

Shawn Messonnier, D.V.M.

Republic of Texas Press
an imprint of
Wordware Publishing, Inc.

Library of Congress Cataloging-in-Publication Data

Messonnier, Shawn.
Exotic pets : a veterinary guide for owners / Shawn Messonnier.
p. cm.
Includes index.
ISBN 1-55622-381-1
1. Wild animals as pets. 2. Pets. I. Title.
SF413.M48 1994
636.088'7--dc20 94-21728
CIP

Printed in the United States of America

ISBN 1-55622-381-1

10 9 8 7 6 5 4 3 2 1

9409

All inquiries for volume purchases of this book should be addressed to Wordware Publishing, Inc., at 1506 Capital Avenue, Plano, Texas 75074. Telephone inquiries may be made by calling:

(214) 423-0090

Contents

Acknowledgements

Writing a book, no matter how fun and exciting, is a major undertaking. In preparing this book, words of thanks go out to the following people:

To my wife Sandy, for her support and understanding. Writing a book requires some amount of time spent away from home. Her love and patience are not forgotten;

To my office staff, for putting up with my frequent interruptions at the computer so that I could complete the manuscript on time;

To the many veterinarians, groomers, breeders, and pet store employees, who refer most, if not all, of the exotic pets we treat at our hospital. Their confidence in us is gratifying; we are glad we can offer owners of these special pets the same high quality care we offer dogs and cats;

To the owners of exotic pets; I'm forever grateful to those who seek quality care for their pets. The questions that these owners frequently asked was the driving force behind the development of this book;

Finally, to the good folks at Wordware Publishing, Inc., especially Mary Goldman. This book was a new venture for them; I am grateful for their confidence in my writing and the need to educate pet owners about their special pets.

To all of you who read this book; I hope that you will be better pet owners as a result of my undertaking. I firmly believe that an educated pet owner is a better pet owner. Pets of educated owners usually are happier, healthier, and live longer. Good luck!

Chapter 1

An Introduction to Reptile Pets

Reptiles are popular pets. Some people want to own them to be different (which should never be the sole reason for owning any pet), some like that the cost of veterinary care is lower than for dogs and cats (this is often but not always true), and many people who don't have the time to devote to a dog or cat enjoy the relatively "maintenance-free" appeal of a snake, iguana, or turtle.

Before purchasing a reptile, the owner must ask himself several questions:

1. Do I want a pet just to look at or do I want to handle and socialize it?

While many reptiles, especially those purchased as captive-born infants, allow owners to handle them, others do not. Many of the more exotic species (which are not discussed in this book) such as chameleons do not allow handling and react aggressively or become severely stressed. As a rule, if you want a pet to snuggle with, a reptile is not for you. If, on the other hand, you want an animal you can display, a reptile deserves your consideration.

2. How much time can I devote to my pet?

I believe that all pets require *at least* 15 minutes of observation by the owner each day. The owner who fails to pay at least this much attention to his pet won't detect early signs of disease and is neglecting his responsibility as a pet owner. Most reptiles need to be fed and watered daily, and often the cage needs to be cleaned daily as well. The owner who intends to put his reptile in a cage and observe it only once in a while should seriously consider his decision to care for this type of pet.

3. Can I afford proper medical care?

ALL reptiles need to be examined immediately after purchase (within 48 hours) and at least annually by a reptile veterinarian. Doing this allows early detection of disease. With very rare exception, exotic pets usually don't act sick or show any indication of illness until they are *very sick*! My staff is trained to gently tell pet owners who call inquiring about what they can do for their sick pets that any sick exotic pet isn't just sick: it's dying! Regular veterinary care and an informed pet owner can greatly reduce illness and death in these pets (as well as the overall cost of medical care).

4. Can I make or buy the correct habitat (home) for my reptile?

At a minimum, reptiles require a 10-gallon glass aquarium, two pieces of Astroturf to line the bottom of the aquarium, a source of heat, and a source of UV light. While not expensive or difficult to assemble, an improper environment is the second most common source of disease and captivity problems encountered in reptiles (an improper diet is the most common problem).

Reptiles do get sick, and preventing illness is definitely preferred to treatment. As an introduction to reptile diseases, the reader needs to understand that reptiles hide signs of illness quite well. This is called the "preservation response." In the wild, if an animal showed signs of illness every time it felt bad, it would easily be attacked by predators or even members of its own group. Therefore, these animals don't appear ill until the illness is actually quite advanced. Our pet reptiles still retain this "wild" characteristic. *A sick reptile is a dying reptile!* It's very important to take your pet to the veterinarian at the FIRST sign of illness. Waiting to see if things get better, or treating it with over-the-counter medications, especially those sold at pet stores, only delays proper treatment and often results in high veterinary bills and a dead reptile! We can do many things for sick reptiles, but we need to start treatment early.

Surgery is occasionally performed on reptiles to correct intestinal obstructions or egg binding, amputate limbs and tails, repair skin wounds, and remove tumors. Surgery is safe, especially if isoflurane gas anesthesia is used. While the basic surgical principles that apply to dogs and cats also apply to reptiles, there are important differences. One such difference is the healing time of sutured skin. With most pets, sutures (stitches) are removed seven to ten days after the surgery. With reptiles, it's not uncommon to leave sutures alone for six weeks or more. Only a veterinarian with expertise in treating reptiles should be consulted for medical or surgical advice.

Chapter 2

The Green Iguana

General Information

Green iguanas are probably the most popular lizards kept as pets. Readily available, they are also fairly inexpensive, especially when acquired at a small size (50-100 grams). Mature males (two years and older) have larger and more pronounced femoral pores on the inner aspects of the thighs than females. These pores are the openings of glands that are used in marking behaviors. Iguanas can be probed (in their cloacal area, which is the common opening of the digestive, urinary, and genital tracts) by a veterinarian to determine their sex. Under proper conditions, adults can grow to weigh several pounds and grow to six feet in length. Therefore, proper provisions must be made for a larger enclosure as the pet ages. Sexual maturity is reached by two years of age. Females can lay eggs without a male, although the eggs will be infertile and won't hatch. With proper care, your iguana can live ten to fifteen years.

Anatomical Interests

1. Iguanas do not have diaphragms; they use muscles located between their ribs (intercostal muscles) for breathing.

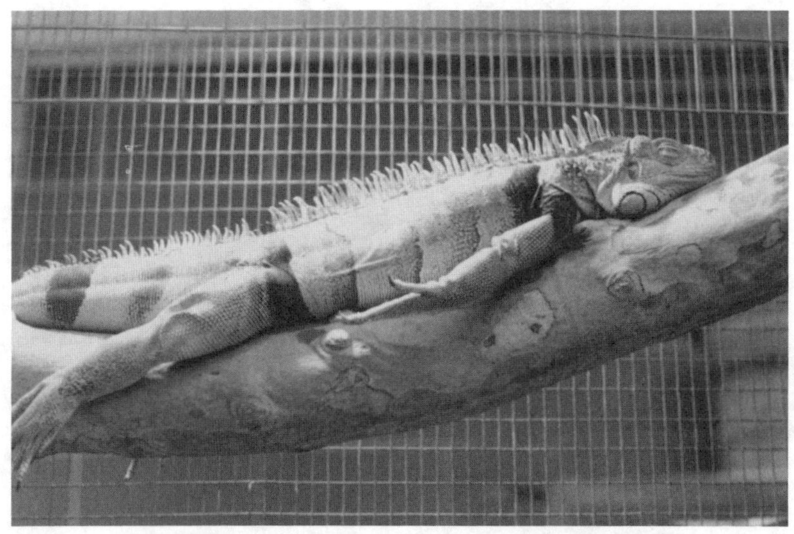

2. Iguanas have a three-chambered heart.
3. Iguanas have a renal portal blood system, where blood from the hindlimbs is filtered by the kidneys before reaching the general circulation.
4. Iguanas excrete uric acid as their main waste product of protein metabolism. This allows them to adapt to desert environments where water supply might be restricted.
5. Males have two reproductive organs called hemipenes.
6. Iguanas have a cloaca which receives secretions from the urinary, gastrointestinal, and reproductive systems.
7. Iguanas' skin is covered with scales and is usually shed in patches, unlike snakes, which usually shed their skin in one piece.
8. Unlike many reptiles, iguanas have a urinary bladder.

Selecting Your Pet

Most owners will buy their iguanas locally from a pet store, although mail ordering from reptile breeders is also common. If you buy a pet through the mail, make sure you know what you're getting! Ask about a guarantee if the pet isn't what you want.

Ideally, you should acquire a young captive-raised animal. Older imported animals are harder to tame, may harbor internal parasites, and often suffer from the stress of captivity. Avoid sick-looking animals. Don't try to be a "Good Samaritan." Remember that with sick exotic pets, if it looks sick it's really dying! Trying to nurse a sick iguana back to health after purchasing it will rarely work. Just the stress of a new environment is often enough to kill a sick iguana. Start out right with a healthy pet. Avoid lizards that appear skinny, have loose skin or sunken eyes, and appear inactive or lethargic. A healthy iguana is usually bright green, active, and alert. The vent or cloaca should be clean and free of wetness or stool. If you can *gently* open the mouth (tapping lightly on the snout with a finger often works), there should be a small amount of clear saliva present, and a bright pink tongue and oral cavity. Mucus that is cloudy or has a "cottage cheese" appearance is a sign of mouth rot, as is redness or pinpoint hemorrhages on the mucus membranes. Of course, your new pet should be examined by a reptile veterinarian within 48 hours of purchase, so if you can't examine the mouth, he can. Even with pet stores, always inquire about the guarantee in case the iguana is found to be unhealthy.

The First Veterinary Visit

Your pet's first visit to a reptile veterinarian should include determining the animal's weight, as well as checking for lumps and bumps. The animal is examined for signs of dehydration and starvation. A fecal test is done to check for internal parasites. Many veterinarians consider all iguanas (even those bred in captivity) to have pinworms, so your iguana may be routinely dewormed. The oral cavity is examined for signs of infectious stomatitis (mouth rot). No vaccines are required for iguanas. Most of the visit will probably be a question-and-answer session. We spend an average of 30 minutes with all new exotic pet owners and give them a handout as well as suggest several good books to read on the care of their new pet. If all turns out well, your iguana will be given a clean bill of health. Like all pets, iguanas should be examined annually and have their stool tested for parasites annually.

Housing

While the smaller juvenile pets often do well in 10- or 20-gallon aquarium, the larger iguanas must be moved to more comfortable enclosures. These can often be purchased or built by the pet owner.

Substrate, or cage lining material, should be easy to clean and nontoxic to the iguana. Newspaper, butcher paper, towels, or Astroturf are recommended. Astroturf is preferred by many reptile owners. Acquire two pieces of turf and cut them to fit the bottom of the cage. With two pieces, one is always in the cage and one is kept outside the cage and is always clean. When the turf inside the cage becomes soiled, you'll always have a clean, dry piece to replace it. Clean the soiled turf with ordinary soap and water (avoid harsher products unless your reptile veterinarian OKs them), thoroughly rinse it, and hang it to dry so it will be ready to use at the next cage cleaning.

Alfalfa pellets can also be used for bedding and are often eaten by the iguana, which is acceptable. Avoid sand, gravel, wood shavings, corn cob material, walnut shells, and cat litter, as these are not only difficult to clean but can cause impactions if eaten on purpose or accidentally should the food become covered by these substrates. Cedar wood shavings are toxic to reptiles!

Iguanas enjoy natural branches. Make sure they are secure and won't fall onto the lizard and injure it. Ideally, the branch should slope from the bottom of the enclosure to the top and end near a heat source so the iguana can bask. Rocks (large ones) in the cage also allow for basking. A hiding place is appreciated by all reptiles and should be available. Artificial plants can be arranged to provide a hiding place, as can clay pots, cardboard boxes, and other containers that provide a secure area.

A heat source is necessary for all reptiles, which are cold-blooded and need a range of temperatures to regulate their internal body temperature. Ideally, the cage should be set up so that a heat gradient is established, with one end warmer than the other end. In this way, the iguana can move around its environment and warm or cool itself as needed. In order to establish and maintain the proper temperature gradient, owners should purchase two thermometers and place one at the cooler end of the cage and one at the warmer end. The cooler end of the cage should be 70-75 degrees Fahrenheit, while the warmer end should be 90-95 degrees. A convenient, inexpensive, and safe way to do this is to supply a focal heat source. A 100-watt incandescent bulb with a reflector hood works well. This heat source should be placed *outside* and above one end of the cage, which should be covered by a screen top to prevent the iguana from escaping or burning itself on the bulb. At night, heat isn't necessary as long as the temperature remains at 65-70 degrees.

A good way to allow the animal to bask is to place the bulb and hood at one end of the cage and arrange a branch or perching (basking) area near the light. This allows the animal psychological stimulation (provided by climbing) as well as a safe heat source.

A popular form of offering heat for reptiles is the infamous "Hot Rock" or "Sizzle Rock." These devices are dangerous and should be avoided! There are several reasons for this warning. With the exception of very small reptiles, they will not supply enough heat for the pet. Even if one can find a large enough rock, it is hard to find one that is safe. There are many stories of iguanas burning themselves, often severely, from prolonged contact with this (and other) heat sources. Why an animal would not remove itself from a dangerously hot appliance is unknown, but it is not uncommon for reptiles to sustain severe, even fatal, burns from a Hot Rock (or an exposed 100-watt bulb). Therefore, the Hot Rocks and similar devices are not recommended!

Heating pads can be used underneath the cage, at one end of the enclosure. Two words of advice: first, make sure the pad adequately warms that part of the cage. Second, make sure it doesn't overheat the cage or you'll have a greenhouse effect. Many experts recommend elevating the cage about 1 inch off the ground with blocks and then sliding the heating pad underneath the cage. If heating pads are used, the top of the cage must not be opened (it should be covered) or too much heat will be lost. Instead, a few small holes can be cut at the top and along the lower part of the cage for ventilation and thermoregulation.

Heating tape or coils of the variety used to warm the soil for plant protection are another possibility. However, these need to be buried in the soil (which really isn't recommended as a cage substrate) and can cause harm if exposed.

Finally, room space heaters can be used if the room cools down too much at night. They probably shouldn't be the only heat source, as they don't allow for a cooler area of the cage.

A source of vitamin D must also be provided. As discussed below, lack of vitamin D is a major cause of metabolic bone disease. While vitamin D certainly should be provided in the diet, it is still necessary to provide it to the iguana by using UV light. In addition to providing vitamin D, these lights, as well as full spectrum lights, also seem to have a positive impact on the psychological well-being of the pet.

The best recommendation is to provide light and UV light using a two-bulb fixture. Ideally, the UV light should emit light in the UV-B range (290-320 nanometers). Combining a black light (such as one from General Electric) with a Vita-Lite, Chroma-50, or Colortone-50 in a two-bulb fixture seems to meet the needs of the iguana. Other acceptable UV lights include the TL-09 and TL-12 from Philips, and the Ultra-Vitalux from Osram. The plant black light from Sylvania, the Gro-Lux, definitely needs to be combined with a UV light. The UV output of these lights decreases with age; many recommend replacing the lights at least yearly, and some (including myself) suggest every six months. For UV light to work, it must reach the pet in an unfiltered form, which means that you must make sure there is no glass or plastic interposed between the pet and the light.

Plant lights (without additional UV light supplementation) and poster-type black lights are not recommended, as they don't provide much light in the required 290-320 nanometer range.

Exposing the pet to direct, *unfiltered* sunlight is always a good idea, as the UV portion of sunlight is filtered by plastic or glass. Several words of caution should be mentioned, however. First, putting a glass aquarium in direct sunlight can easily cause the aquarium to get dangerously hot (similar to leaving a child or pet in a closed car in the summer). Second, taking the pet out of its normal cage is fine, but care must be taken to prevent its escape or attack by other pets. An outdoor cage constructed of wood and wire screen is an acceptable method of exposing reptiles to sunlight. Finally, some reptiles become aggressive immediately following exposure to sunlight. Care should be used when handling reptiles immediately after a "sunbath."

The iguana should receive about twelve hours of light and twelve hours of darkness each day. Make sure the cage or room is warm enough when the lights are turned out.

Infrared heat lamps can be used outside of the cage during the dark periods if needed.

Common sense dictates that fresh water be available at all times.

Finally, iguanas appreciate a "private" area where they can hide. A clay pot or shoe box usually works well.

Feeding

There is currently much misinformation concerning the feeding of exotic pets. This misinformation is presented in books available for purchase by the public. These books, supposedly written by "experts," encourage iguana owners to feed their pets only insects, insects and fruit, insects and fruit cocktail, dog food, cat food, or even ice cream. Improper feeding is the major cause of the number one disease seen in green iguanas, metabolic bone disease. It is most important that owners of exotic pets provide their pets the proper diet and environment. Doing just these two things will prevent most of the diseases commonly seen.

In feeding your green iguana, it is important to understand how these reptiles eat in the wild. The green iguana is a reptile found in Central and South America and Mexico. Studies in Panama found that iguanas eat mainly vegetable matter, including the fruit, leaves, and flowers of certain bushes, trees, and vines. Their feedings occur in frequent, small meals. This means that iguanas are mainly herbivorous, although they eat a small amount of insects too. This diet is mainly fiber and plant protein and contains very little fat. The hindgut of the iguana is highly specialized to allow fiber digestion, similar to the stomach compartments of cattle.

Feeding your iguana requires two different feeding regimens, one for juvenile pets (less than two years of age) and one for adults (over two years of age), as the requirements are slightly different for growing animals than for adults. For juveniles, 80% of the diet should be plant-based and 20%

protein-based. For adult iguanas, 90% of the diet should be plant-based and 10% protein-based. This decrease in protein will ease the workload on the kidneys, whose main function is to decrease nitrogenous (protein) waste. Of the plant matter, most (80%) should be flowers and vegetables, and only 20% should be fruits. Even though iguanas enjoy the sweet taste of fruit, compared with vegetables it is deficient in some minerals and vitamins. Fruit should be considered mainly a treat.

As a rule, anything green and leafy should make up a large part of the diet. Yellow and orange vegetables should also be included. Avoid fiber-rich, vitamin-deficient vegetables including lettuce and celery; their composition is mainly fiber and water with little nutritional value.

Acceptable vegetables include collard greens, mustard greens, turnip greens, alfalfa hay or chow, bok choy, kale, parsley, spinach (in small amounts), bell pepper, green beans, green peas, corn, okra, cactus, various squashes, sweet potatoes, cabbage or broccoli (also in small amounts), and flowers such as carnations, hibiscus, and roses (avoid azaleas as they are toxic).

Vegetables can be cooked or raw (thoroughly wash raw veggies); experiment with your iguana to see if he prefers his vegetables raw or cooked. Flowers can be home-grown or purchased from floral shops. Often, floral shops throw out older, wilting flowers. Since these may be unacceptable for sale to the public, reptile owners can often get them free. Make sure that no chemicals have been applied to the flowers or water.

Fruit can include apples, pears, bananas, grapes, peaches, kiwis, and melons. Fruits that are particularly healthy include figs (which contain calcium), papaya, raspberries, and strawberries.

Appropriate protein sources include crickets, sardines (drained), tofu, hard-boiled eggs, earthworms, and mealworms. Dog food and cat food contain too much vitamin D and fat and should not be given. Reptile pellets, bird pellets, trout chow, and other fish chows are excellent protein sources; feeding these precludes the need for live prey (although you can feed live prey as well, as iguanas often enjoy the psychological stimulation of catching the live prey).

Live prey, such as crickets and worms, should either be raised by the owner or purchased from a pet store or reptile breeder. *Never* feed your iguana insects taken from the family garden. Raising your own insects is easy; the Chicago Herpetological Society has an excellent manual entitled *The Right Way to Feed Insect-Eating Lizards* discussing this topic. If you get your insects from a local pet store, it is a good idea to "nutrient load" them prior to feeding them to your iguana. Keep them in a container and feed the insects finely ground rodent or fish chow. Fish flakes blended with calcium carbonate powder and high protein baby cereal flakes can also be fed to the insects. A slice of orange (for crickets) or sweet potato (for mealworms) can serve as a water source for the insects. Insects should be fed for at least a few days before offering them to your iguana. Prior to feeding your iguana, lightly sprinkle the insects with a good multivitamin powder (available at pet stores or from your veterinarian).

It is recommended by many veterinarians to *lightly* sprinkle all the food offered to the iguana with a calcium powder (calcium gluconate, lactate, or carbonate). Weekly, a light sprinkling of a good reptile vitamin on the food is also recommended. A light dusting means just that; oversupplementation can cause problems. Think of a light sprinkling the same way you would lightly salt food for yourself!

Juvenile iguanas should be fed daily, while adult iguanas can be fed every other day. These are just guidelines, as many adults will eat daily.

Fresh water in a crock that won't easily tip over should be available at all times. Iguanas will not only drink from the water bowl but will often bathe in it as well (although it is perfectly acceptable to mist the iguana with water a few times a week too). Make sure the water stays clean; many reptiles love to eliminate in their water bowl as well as drink from it.

In summary, iguanas eat mainly plant-based food. Variety is the key. Don't let your iguana get "hooked" on just one or two favorite items. Feed many items in small portions. Make sure the food is the right size for your pet: smaller animals need their food finely chopped. As with all pets, fresh vegetables and fruits are preferred, frozen is second best, and canned is least desirable. Make up about a week's worth and refrigerate or freeze the remaining portions for your convenience. Remember, your pet is what it eats, and when feeding insects, your pet is what its prey eats, so feed the prey properly, too!

Common Diseases

The most common iguana diseases occur as a result of owner misinformation. Improper feeding and improper environment (housing) contribute to most of the problems seen by reptile veterinarians. Even many infections are secondary to poor environment and diet. Therefore, with proper knowledge, some of the diseases frequently seen in iguanas can be prevented.

Metabolic Bone Disease

This disease is also called nutritional osteodystrophy and nutritional secondary hyperparathyroidism. The condition results from a lack of calcium and/or vitamin D in the diet.

Calcium is needed for many things in a pet's body. The correct levels of calcium need to be maintained in the bloodstream; otherwise, seizures and cardiac arrest may occur. The body has several intricate physiological mechanisms to maintain a normal level of calcium in the blood. Dietary calcium is absorbed by the intestines under the influence of vitamin D, which can be obtained through the diet or through UV light (including sunlight). Calcium is stored in the bones under the influence of a hormone called calcitonin. When the blood calcium level decreases, several things happen: the kidneys excrete less calcium in the urine, more calcium is absorbed by the intestines, and calcium is removed from the bones under the influence of another hormone called parathyroid hormone.

When the diet contains inadequate amounts of calcium or vitamin D, over a period of time too much calcium is taken from the bones. The result is a bone with a thin outer layer (cortex) which is very prone to fracturing (breaking). While all bones in the body can be affected, early signs are usually seen in the lower jawbone, or mandible, which becomes rubbery and pliable (a slang term for this disease is "rubber jaw"). Even though the blood calcium level usually remains normal, the animal can show signs of illness. The most commonly seen signs include weakness, lethargy, and anorexia (refusal to eat).

Iguanas with metabolic bone disease often have swellings of the jaws or legs. (I usually see swollen rear limbs as opposed to swollen front limbs.) Many owners mistakenly assume that these swollen limbs (often more easily noticed than the swollen mandible) represent an increase in muscle. This swollen tissue is actually fibrous connective tissue that forms as a consequence of this disease. A more severe sign occasionally noticed is an inability of the animal to walk with its back legs. This is often a result of weakness and not true paralysis caused by a fracture of the weakened spinal column (vertebral fractures). The veterinarian can tell exactly what is preventing the pet from using its rear legs after performing a thorough physical examination and radiographing (taking X-rays) of the pet.

If this condition is a result of an improper diet or environment, what foods are the most common offending items? Well, meat is known to contain very little calcium. Any animal or person fed a diet composed entirely of meat is going to develop metabolic bone disease. Iguanas maintained entirely on crickets and fruit cocktail (unfortunately a common scenario) also are eating a calcium-deficient diet. Most of these pets are usually not receiving any mineral or vitamin supplementation, or any UV light. You can see how this disease can either be prevented or caused by the owner.

Clinical signs of metabolic bone disease include swelling and flexibility of the mandible (lower jaw). While this is the earliest sign of this disease, most owners don't detect the problem at this stage. Typically, the pet isn't brought in for a checkup until it becomes lethargic, stops eating, and can't move. In my experience, if the pet is still eating and somewhat active, the chance for a cure is much better.

A complete examination is needed. Often, these animals also have mouth rot and are infected with internal parasites. A good exam and radiographs (X-rays) can provide a lot of information. The rule in medicine is to "treat the pet, not the disease." Therefore, individuals with parasites, mouth rot, or other problems need these addressed as well as the metabolic bone disease.

Iguanas that are still active and eating can be treated at home. Injections of calcium gluconate are given by the owner in the pet's peritoneal (abdominal) cavity; most owners can be easily taught this procedure. A UV light is supplied as well. Often, a vitamin injection is also given. I try not to correct the improper diet until the animal has recovered from the disease; then, the diet is slowly changed. Recovery, if it occurs, should be seen after four to six weeks of injections. Owners are instructed to remove all objects from the cage except the food and water bowls. The bones of these sick pets are very fragile and can easily fracture if the iguana falls off a basking area or if a branch falls onto the pet.

Iguanas that are lethargic and not eating always have a guarded prognosis, but treatment should always be attempted. I advise owners that while many pets that are severely ill will die, about 20% won't, and since we can't tell which category any pet falls into, we should attempt treatment. These animals are very sick and need to be hospitalized. They are placed in an incubator and given intraperitoneal fluids. We also force feed them in an attempt to get them to start eating. If improvement is to be seen, it usually occurs within three days of intensive care.

After the disease is cured, the owners are shown how to slowly correct the diet; UV light and vitamins and minerals are provided as well.

Hypervitaminosis D

While hypovitaminosis D (too little vitamin D) is one of the causes of metabolic bone disease, too much vitamin D is also harmful. This usually occurs when owners either over-supplement with vitamins and minerals (only a light sprinkling is needed on the food a few times a week) or feed dog food or cat food to their iguanas (both contain way too much vitamin D, as well as too much fat and protein).

Clinical signs are nonspecific and resemble many diseases; often, only anorexia and lethargy are seen. Radiographs occasionally reveal calcification of blood vessels or body organs. Blood tests for calcium usually reveal a dangerously high calcium level.

Treatment includes correcting the diet and hospitalization to correct the high calcium level. Fluids, corticosteroids, and calcitonin hormone are given to lower the calcium levels in the blood. As with dogs and cats with this disease, treatment is not always successful. Prevention is once again the best medicine.

Infectious Stomatitis

This condition is more commonly known by the term "mouth rot." The disease is almost always caused by bacteria. While many bacteria are capable of causing the problem, *Pseudomonas* and *Aeromonas* are the most common. Many doctors feel that this disease is always a secondary one, which means something must set it off. These doctors feel this way because Pseudomonas and Aeromonas bacteria are often normally present in a reptile's environment and body. Certainly a filthy environment is a common cause of this disease. Other stressors than can cause the disease include internal parasites, poor diet, improper environment and improper environmental temperature (low body temperature in any animal decreases the ability of the body's immune system to fight off infection), shipping (as when a pet is purchased and brought into the owner's home), too little or too much handling, a too humid or too dry environment, and almost any other type of stress! The stress is not always identified, but the pet should undergo a thorough diagnostic workup (treat the pet, not the disease!).

Early signs that often go unnoticed by owners are small, pinpoint areas of hemorrhage inside the oral cavity (roof or floor of the mouth and gums). The later stages of the disease reveal a large amount of frothy, bubbly mucus or a cottage cheese-type material in the mouth. Many animals in these later stages are anorectic (not eating) and lethargic.

Diagnosis is fairly easy and is made by observation of the oral cavity. All cases and suspected cases of mouth rot should be cultured. Pseudomonas and Aeromonas are found in many normal reptiles, so just finding them on a culture doesn't always means the pet has or will develop mouth rot. However, any heavy growth of either bacteria on a culture should probably be treated.

A culture gives several pieces of information. First, it confirms whether or not bacteria or fungi are seen in the mucus (this is especially helpful in "borderline" cases, where the doctor feels the amount of mucus in the mouth is abnormal but isn't quite sure if it's necessarily anything to worry about). Second, the culture tells us specifically which bacteria or fungus is present and causing the disease. Finally, the culture tells us which drug (antibiotic) should be used to treat the infection.

Treatment varies with the severity of the illness. Pets that are not eating and are lethargic need hospitalization. During hospitalization, these animals are given fluids (to prevent dehydration as well as to prevent toxic levels of antibiotics from damaging the kidneys), kept warm in an incubator, and force-fed. (All sick animals need to be fed to prevent the harmful effects seen with anorexia, such as muscle wasting and depressed immune systems.)

While awaiting the culture results, the iguanas are started on injectable antibiotics. The oral cavity is treated with a topical antibacterial medication, such as Betadine, chlorhexidine, hydrogen peroxide, or Silvadene. Atropine injections are given if the mucus is thick; vitamin injections are given routinely, as many iguanas are on a vitamin-deficient diet. Vitamin C also seems to help in many cases of mouth rot.

The prognosis of mouth rot depends upon several factors. If the animal is still eating and not lethargic, the prognosis is good. If signs are caught very early when only the pinpoint hemorrhages are seen, the chance for recovery is excellent. Those animals that are lethargic and not eating have a more guarded prognosis. Secondary problems, such as internal parasites, must also be treated. Once the animal has recovered, diet and environment are changed as needed.

Abscesses

Unlike mammals, birds and reptiles usually don't form liquid pus. When these pets form abscesses, they appear as hard lumps (like tumors). This makes it difficult if not impossible to diagnose an abscess, as an aspirate of the lump is usually unrewarding (in mammals, an aspirate usually reveals liquid pus). Diagnosis and treatment are the same, namely opening the abscess under anesthesia, cleaning it out, and using antibiotics based on culturing the material in the abscess.

Avascular Necrosis

Iguanas often have a condition called avascular necrosis, which occurs in the digits (fingers and toes) or tail. Basically, a blood vessel becomes constricted and the blood supply is stopped. When the tail or digit doesn't receive blood, it undergoes necrosis and dies. These dead areas appear darker than the surrounding tissue. Left untreated, the necrosis can spread up the tail or digit.

The exact cause isn't always known, but can include septicemia (blood poisoning), mycotoxicosis (infection with mold), mycobacteriosis (infection with a tuberculosis-type bacterium), fungal infections, or skin that is retained after molting.

Treatment is simple when caught early; the affected area is amputated. The tail usually grows back if it isn't sutured (sewn closed).

Cystic Calculi

Commonly called bladder stones, these occur when minerals from the diet form crystals which then form stones. Usually these are composed of uric acid, which can result from a diet that contains too much protein.

Blood in the droppings, as well as abdominal swelling, can be a sign of this malady. An examination and radiographs allow the diagnosis to be confirmed. Surgical removal of the stone is needed, as is fluid therapy to prevent kidney damage; the diet should be corrected if possible to prevent future stones from forming.

Parasites

Reptiles get "worms" just like dogs and cats. Even captive-bred animals can become infected with intestinal parasites. Like many reptile veterinarians, I routinely treat iguanas for pinworms, a common parasite of green iguanas. An annual stool exam is needed to make sure the pet remains free of parasites.

Kidney Failure

As with so many pets, kidney failure can cause death in iguanas. These pets are usually older, and often the kidney failure is due to the same high-protein diet that causes bladder stones. As with mammals, kidney failure is often irreversible. With dogs and cats, we can often sustain life for a period of time. With exotic pets, too often the problem is not diagnosed until it's too late. Treatment, when attempted, is with hospitalization and aggressive fluid and antibiotic therapy.

Antibiotic Toxicity

Many antibiotics commonly used in pets and people are toxic to reptiles if given in the wrong amount or dosage frequency. This is yet another important reason to make sure your veterinarian is qualified to treat reptiles.

Salmonella

While box turtles are infamous for carrying salmonella bacteria, any reptile can harbor this organism. Recently, there have been reports of illness in people who own iguanas. This bacteria can cause severe gastrointestinal disease or septicemia (blood poisoning). Many animals and people carry the bacteria without showing any clinical signs, yet shed the bacteria in their feces, which can infect others.

Prevention, through proper hygiene, is the best way to control the disease. Since most animals that carry salmonella are not ill, they usually require no treatment (which often fails to kill the bacteria anyway).

Dystocia

Dystocia means "difficult birth." It occasionally occurs when an egg has trouble passing through the birth canal. When a reptile cannot pass an egg, it must have medical intervention within a reasonable period of time or it will die.

In order to suspect dystocia (also called egg retention), you need to know if your pet is a male or female. Probing of the cloacal area by a veterinarian, while not always 100% accurate, is reliable. With male pets, the probe can be inserted about twice as far as in females.

If the animal is known to be female, diagnosing the condition is a bit easier. Often one or several eggs have already passed, yet the iguana continues to strain as if trying to pass the remaining eggs. Signs often seen with dystocia, even if no eggs have been passed, include refusal to eat, not moving very much, and possibly a personality change (the pet may be less active or more irritable). These signs are not unique to dystocia and can be seen with many reptile diseases.

Definitive diagnosis usually requires radiographs (X-rays); unless the shells are not calcified, the eggs are readily visible.

The cause of the dystocia is often unknown. However, a poor diet, incorrect environmental temperature, and internal diseases are all contributing factors. For whatever reason, the uterus fails to expel the eggs and they get stuck. Occasionally, the eggs are too big to pass through the cloaca, and this causes the dystocia.

The objective of treatment is to relieve the dystocia and allow the iguana to pass the eggs. Depending upon the severity of the case, warming the pet, administering injectable medications, or even surgery can correct the problem.

Chapter 3

The Ball Python

The royal python has been nicknamed the ball python due to its inclination to roll up into a tight ball when scared. This ball position is a good defense position: the head is out of harm's way, and a ball of snake coils is larger and more difficult to kill and eat than a linear arrangement of the snake's body.

While much of the information presented in this chapter applies to many species of pet snakes, each species has its own dietary, environmental, and behavioral idiosyncrasies. The reader is urged to contact references regarding the specific species of snake. The ball python was chosen to be

the "representative" snake, as it is the snake most commonly seen in the author's practice.

The ball python is probably the most common snake purchased as a pet. They are relatively inexpensive, and except for a very rare individual are nonaggressive and easily handled. These good points unfortunately are offset by some negative attributes. Wild caught specimens often harbor parasites (external and internal) and are infected with mouth rot. Even healthy snakes have one major drawback: they are often very reluctant to eat, especially when first acquired. It is almost "normal" for a newly acquired ball python to go without eating for several months! Getting them to eat is difficult, often expensive, and quite a challenge. This drawback must be seriously considered by every potential snake owner prior to purchase, but especially if the new pet is a ball python.

Unless captive bred (which is always the ideal situation when dealing with exotic pets), imported snakes come from Togo and Ghana in Africa. Females and males look identical. Some people feel that the cloacal spurs on males are more prominent. A veterinarian can carefully probe the cloacal area to determine the sex of your new pet. Hatchlings are about a foot long and grow to about 3 feet by 3 years of age. At maturity (reached in 3-5 years), adults reach 5-6 feet in length. Depending upon their care, ball pythons can live 10-20 years.

Anatomical Interests

1. Most snakes have only one functional, simple lung (usually the right lung).
2. Snakes have a cloaca, a common opening for the urinary, digestive, and genital tracts.
3. Snakes have no limbs; many people feel the spurs that are present on some snakes represent vestigial limbs.
4. Snakes have numerous pairs of ribs.

5. Snakes have a three-chambered heart.
6. Snakes have no diaphragm; this prevents coughing and airway clearance, and snakes with simple respiratory infections easily develop pneumonia because of this. Respiratory infections in reptiles are always more serious than similar infections in mammals.
7. Males have two reproductive organs called hemipenes.
8. Snakes have spectacles instead of eyelids.

Selecting Your Pet

Most owners buy their snakes locally from a pet store, although mail ordering from reptile breeders is also common. If you buy a pet through the mail, make sure you know what you're getting! Ask about a guarantee if the pet isn't what you want.

Ideally, you should acquire a young captive-raised animal. Older imported animals are harder to tame, may harbor internal parasites, and often suffer from the stress of captivity. Additionally, older imported pythons are notoriously difficult to feed. It's not uncommon for owners to spend $200 or more for several veterinary visits in an attempt to get their snake to start eating. Avoid sick-looking animals. Don't try to be a "Good Samaritan." Remember that with sick exotic pets, if it looks sick, it's really dying! Trying to nurse a sick python back to health after purchasing it will rarely work. Just the stress of a new environment is often enough to kill a sick snake. Start out right with a healthy pet. Avoid snakes that appear skinny, have loose skin or sunken eyes, and seem inactive or lethargic. A healthy snake is usually round and not sunken in at the sides, has a shiny color, and is active and alert. When handling the snake you should get the impression that it is strong and has good muscle tone. Snakes that do not resist handling are often ill. The vent or cloaca should be clean and free of wetness or stool. If you can *gently* open the mouth (a soft, clean, rubber spatula works well), there should be a small amount of clear saliva present and a bright pink tongue and oral cavity. Mucus that is cloudy or has a "cottage cheese" appearance is a sign of mouth rot, as is redness or pinpoint hemorrhages on the mucus membranes. The eyes should be clear; cloudy eyes usually indicate the snake is about to shed. As you examine the eyes, check for mites, which are tiny black dots that often move. Make sure no lumps or bumps are present; simply running your hands slowly down the snake's body will allow you to detect any swellings. While not a sign of illness, shedding is very stressful to snakes and it would be best to purchase a snake that is not about to shed. Of course, your new pet should be examined by a reptile veterinarian within 48 hours of purchase. Even with pet stores, always inquire about the guarantee in case the snake is found to be unhealthy.

The First Veterinary Visit

Your snake's first visit to the reptile veterinarian should include determining the animal's weight, as well as checking for lumps and bumps. The animal is examined for signs of dehydration and starvation. A fecal test is done to check for internal parasites. A snake's feces is often a hard "ball" of fecal matter; analyzing this material gives little useful information. A colonic wash, similar to an enema, will allow your veterinarian to accurately check for internal parasites. Common snake parasites include protozoa and lungworms. The oral cavity is examined for signs of infectious stomatitis (mouth rot). No vaccines are required for snakes. Most of the visit will probably be a question-and-answer session. We spend an average of 30 minutes with all new owners of exotic pets and give them a handout, as well as suggest several good books to read. If all turns out well, your python will be given a clean bill of health. Like all pets, ball pythons should be examined and have their stool tested for parasites annually.

Housing

While many smaller snakes often do well in 10- or 20-gallon aquarium, it won't be long before your snake outgrows this temporary home. A larger, more comfortable environment will need to be provided. These can often be purchased or built by the pet owner. As a rule, the snake should be able to stretch out comfortably and move around.

Substrate, or cage lining material, should be easy to clean and nontoxic to the python. Newspaper, butcher paper, towels, or Astroturf are recommended. Astroturf is preferred by many reptile owners. Acquire two pieces of turf and cut them to fit the bottom of the cage. With two pieces, one is always in the cage and one is kept outside the cage and is always clean. When the turf inside the cage becomes soiled, you'll always have a clean, dry piece to replace it. Clean the soiled turf with ordinary soap and water (avoid harsher products unless your reptile veterinarian OKs them), thoroughly rinse it, and hang it to dry.

Avoid sand, gravel, wood shavings, corn cob material, walnut shells, and cat litter, as these are not only difficult to clean but can cause impactions if eaten on purpose or accidentally should the food become covered by these substrates. Cedar wood shavings are toxic to snakes!

Natural branches are a nice addition to the python's habitat. Make sure they are secure and won't fall onto the pet and injure it. Ideally, the branch should slope from the bottom of the enclosure to the top and end near a heat source so the snake can bask. Rocks (large ones) in the cage also allow for basking. A hiding place is appreciated by all reptiles and should be available. Artificial plants can be arranged to provide a hiding place, as can clay pots, cardboard boxes, and other containers that provide a secure area.

A heat source is necessary for all reptiles, which are cold-blooded and need a variety of temperatures to regulate their internal body temperature. Ideally, the cage should be set up so that a heat gradient is established, with one end warmer than the other end. In this way, the python can move around in its environment and warm or cool itself as needed. In order to establish and maintain the proper temperature gradient, owners should purchase two thermometers and place one at the cooler end of the cage and one at the warmer end. The cooler end of the cage should be 70-75 degrees Fahrenheit, while the warmer end should be 90-95 degrees. A convenient, inexpensive, and safe way to do this is to supply a focal heat source. A 100-watt incandescent bulb with a reflector hood works well. This heat source should be placed *outside* and above one end of the cage, which should be covered by a screen top to prevent the snake from escaping or burning itself on the bulb. At night, heat isn't necessary as long as the temperature remains at 65-70 degrees.

A good way to allow the animal to bask is to place the bulb and hood at one end of the cage and arrange a branch or perching (basking) area near the light. This allows the animal psychological stimulation (provided by climbing) as well as a safe heat source.

A popular form of offering heat for reptiles is the infamous "Hot Rock" or "Sizzle Rock." These devices are dangerous and should be avoided! There are several reasons for this warning. With the exception of very small reptiles, they will not supply adequate heat for the pet. Even if one can find a large enough rock, it is hard to find one that is safe. There are many stories of snakes burning themselves, often severely, from prolonged contact with this (and other) heat sources. Why an animal would not remove itself from a dangerously hot appliance is unknown, but it is not uncommon for reptiles to sustain severe, even fatal, burns from a Hot Rock (or an exposed 100-watt bulb). Therefore, the Hot Rocks and similar devices are not recommended!

Heating pads can be used underneath the cage, at one end of the enclosure. Two words of advice: first, make sure the pad adequately warms that part of the cage. Second, make sure it doesn't overheat the cage or you'll have a greenhouse effect. Many experts recommend elevating the cage about 1 inch off the ground with blocks and then sliding the heating pad underneath the cage. If heating pads are used, the top of the cage must not be opened (it should be covered) or too much heat will be lost. Instead, a few small holes can be cut at the top and along the lower part of the cage for ventilation and thermoregulation.

Heating tape or coils of the variety used to warm the soil for plant protection are another possibility. However, these need to be buried in the soil (which really isn't recommended as a cage substrate) and can cause harm if exposed.

Finally, room space heaters can be used if the room cools down too much at night. They probably shouldn't be the only heat source, as they don't allow for a cooler area of the cage.

A source of vitamin D must also be provided. While vitamin D is provided in the diet since pythons eat whole prey, it is still necessary to provide vitamin D by using UV light. In addition to providing vitamin D, these lights, as well as full spectrum lights, also seem to have a positive impact on the psychological well-being of the pet.

The best recommendation is to provide light and UV light using a two-bulb fixture. Ideally, the UV light should emit light in the UV-B range (290-320 nanometers). Combining a black light (such as one from General Electric) with a Vita-Lite, Chroma-50, or Colortone-50 in a two-bulb fixture seems to meet the needs of the snake. Other acceptable UV lights include the TL-09 and TL-12 from Philips, and the Ultra-Vitalux from Osram. The plant black light from Sylvania, the Gro-Lux, definitely needs to be combined with a UV light. The UV output of these lights decreases with age; many recommend replacing the lights at least yearly, and some (including myself) suggest every six months. For

UV light to work, it must reach the pet in an unfiltered form, which means that you must make sure there is no glass or plastic interposed between the pet and the light.

Plant lights (without additional UV light supplementation) and poster-type black lights are not recommended, as they don't provide much light in the required 290-320 nanometer range.

Exposing the pet to direct, unfiltered sunlight is always a good idea, as the UV portion of sunlight is filtered by plastic or glass. Several words of caution should be mentioned, however. First, putting a glass aquarium in direct sunlight can easily cause the aquarium to get dangerously hot (similar to leaving a child or pet in a closed car in the summer). Second, taking the pet out of its normal cage is fine, but care must be taken to prevent its escape or attack by other pets. An outdoor cage constructed of wood and wire screen is an acceptable method of exposing reptiles to sunlight. Finally, some reptiles become aggressive immediately following exposure to sunlight. Care should be used when handling reptiles immediately after a "sunbath."

The python should receive about twelve hours of light and twelve hours of darkness each day. Make sure the cage or room is warm enough when the lights are turned out. Infrared heat lamps can be used outside of the cage during the dark periods if needed.

Common sense dictates that fresh water be available at all times. While many snakes will "bathe" in the water, misting the python a few times a week is also acceptable.

Finally, snakes appreciate a "private" area where they can hide. A clay pot or shoe box usually works well.

Feeding

Fresh water in a crock that won't easily tip over should be available at all times. As snakes often bathe and eliminate in the crock as well as drink from it, make sure the water stays clean.

Snakes eat live or killed whole prey. While this simplifies things for snake owners and greatly reduces the chance of dietary-related diseases so commonly seen in other reptiles, it does present a problem. Namely, the owner must provide some type of prey to the snake. If you're squeamish about killing rodents for your snake and then watching it eat the prey, a snake is probably not the pet for you!

Ideally, the python should be provided either a thawed, previously frozen prey item, or a freshly killed one. It is not recommend to feed live prey to snakes for several reasons. First, the prey obviously knows it is prey and unless killed and eaten immediately, it certainly suffers some psychological stress. Second, and surprising for most snake owners, is the fact that *even a small mouse can severely injure and even kill a snake if the snake isn't hungry!* For humane reasons, I recommend feeding dead prey. The only exception would be if the owner knows the snake will immediately kill and eat the prey and the owner will watch the snake do this. Even with this care, there is still a slight possibility of injury to the snake. Unweaned, infant prey (pinkie mice) are safe to feed alive.

The most common prey items are mice and rats. Many ball pythons will not eat these, however, as their diet in the wild consists of gerbils and various African species of rats (which are different from the ones so often offered as food items). As I stated in the introduction to this chapter, ball pythons often refuse to eat for months. Getting one to start eating takes patience and often the assistance (and expense) of a reptile veterinarian. A healthy ball python can go for months without eating with no ill effects. However, a veterinarian needs to examine the snake and run appropriate laboratory tests to make sure the snake is healthy.

To help clients get their snakes to eat, here is my general protocol for the anorectic (not eating) snake:

1. Discuss the environment during the first veterinary visit. If no external heat source or hiding place is available, correct these problems.

2. Examine the snake. I like to make sure the snake is healthy.
3. Examine a freshly collected stool sample obtained from a colonic wash for internal parasites.
4. Treat any diseases that are present.
5. If the snake is ill, I force-feed it during the visit.

If the snake appears healthy and doesn't have any parasites, I query the owners about what they have tried to feed the snake. Newly purchased pythons should be left alone without any handling for two to four weeks so they can acclimate themselves to their new home. Handling newly purchased snakes creates stress, and stress kills exotic pets!

Newly imported snakes, snakes getting ready to shed, and pregnant snakes will not eat; this is normal.

I suggest that owners try the following technique, which has been reprinted with the permission of Phillipe de Vosjoli. This information is excerpted from his booklet, *The General Care and Maintenance of Ball Pythons* (highly recommended for new python owners).

1. At night, introduce one or two live unweaned (fuzzy) rats (fuzzy rats are infants and if fed alive will not harm the snake). If the snake doesn't eat, repeat once a week for at least two more times.
2. If the snake is still not eating, offer a freshly killed gerbil. Repeat this once a week for two more weeks if the snake doesn't eat.
3. If this fails, switch back to the unweaned rats for two more weeks.
4. If no response, try a freshly killed recently weaned rat. If no response, try pinkie mice once a week for two more weeks, then try a freshly killed gerbil again for two weeks.

When trying this program, if prey isn't eaten within 24 hours of offering it, remove it and don't bother the snake until the next feeding.

As a rule, do not handle the snake until it has started feeding.

Never handle a snake within 72 hours of feeding, or you may induce a "feeding frenzy" and get bitten!

If the above steps fail, next try the "brown bag" method:

1. Take a brown grocery bag (paper bag) and punch a few holes in it.
2. Place the snake and an unweaned live rat in it, fold the top of the bag over, and staple shut. Leave in the cage overnight and check in the morning.
3. If no success, try again once weekly for two weeks.
4. If still no success, try the procedure with barely weaned gerbils or a freshly killed adult gerbil.

Yes, this is a lot of work, and yes, you have to be very patient. Most snakes will eat at some point during all of these attempts. Occasionally, I will force-feed a snake to get its gastrointestinal tract going, and often I will use an oral appetite-stimulating medication to induce the snake to eat. Eventually, most healthy snakes will eat. You just need to experiment and find the right prey.

What size prey should a snake generally eat? As a rule, offer one prey item whose circumference is about equal to the snake's circumference at its widest point. Of course, several items of smaller prey can be offered in place of the one larger item.

How often do snakes eat? Generally, the smaller snakes eat once a week and the larger ones eat every 2-4 weeks. This statement is extremely general: if your snake eats every few weeks, you'll soon learn how often to feed it. For health reasons, remove uneaten prey within 24 hours.

You may have to kill the prey yourself, as most snakes prefer fresh prey to thawed, previously frozen items. Carbon *dioxide* (not *monoxide*) canisters can be purchased, and the prey can be placed in a closed container with the carbon dioxide (dry ice may also work). Many owners alternatively place the prey items (one item at a time) in a paper bag and slam the bag against a table. The freshly stunned prey can then be offered immediately, or it can be killed by cutting its throat and frozen for a later feeding (it must be thawed before offering it to the snake).

Many owners raise their own mice, gerbils, or rats instead of purchasing them from pet stores. This allows owners to feed the rodents a nutritious diet prior to feeding them to the snakes. Another option is to purchase rodents from national dealers; your local herp club can offer names and addresses of these dealers.

Yes, this talk about killing prey and cutting throats is gruesome, but if you want a ball python as a pet, this is all necessary. If this makes you uncomfortable, a python is not the pet for you!

Diseases

Infectious Stomatitis

This condition is more commonly known by the term "mouth rot." The disease is almost always caused by bacteria. While many bacteria are capable of causing the problem, *Pseudomonas* and *Aeromonas* are the most common. Many doctors feel that this disease is always a secondary one, which means something must set it off, because Pseudomonas and Aeromonas bacteria are often normally present in a reptile's environment and body. Certainly a filthy environment is a common cause of this disease. Other stressors that can cause the disease include internal parasites, poor diet, improper environment and improper environmental temperature (low body temperature in any animal decreases the ability of the body's immune system to fight off infection), shipping (as when a pet is purchased and brought into the owner's home), too little or too much handling, a too humid or too dry environment, and almost any other type of stress! The cause is not always identified, but the pet should undergo a thorough diagnostic workup (treat the pet, not the disease!).

Early signs that often go unnoticed by owners are small, pinpoint areas of hemorrhage inside the oral cavity (roof or floor of the mouth and gums). The later stages of the disease reveal a large amount of frothy, bubbly mucus or a cottage cheese-type material in the mouth. Many animals in these later stages are anorectic (not eating) and lethargic.

Diagnosis is fairly easy and is made by observation of the oral cavity. All cases and suspected cases of mouth rot should be cultured. Pseudomonas and Aeromonas are found in many normal reptiles, so just finding them on a culture doesn't always means the pet has or will develop mouth rot. However, any heavy growth of either bacteria on culture should probably be treated.

A culture gives several pieces of information. First, it confirms whether or not bacteria or fungi are seen in the mucus. (This is especially helpful in "borderline" cases, where the doctor feels the amount of mucus in the mouth is abnormal, but isn't quite sure if it's necessarily anything to worry about.) Second, the culture tells us specifically which bacteria or fungus is present and causing the disease. Finally, the culture tells us which drug (antibiotic) should be used to treat the infection.

Treatment varies with the severity of the illness. As with many diseases, pets that are not eating and are lethargic need hospitalization. During hospitalization, these animals are given fluids (to prevent dehydration as well as to prevent toxic levels of antibiotics from damaging the kidneys), kept warm in an incubator, and force-fed. (All sick animals need to be fed to prevent the harmful effects seen with anorexia, such as muscle wasting and depressed immune systems.)

While awaiting the culture results, the snakes are started on injectable antibiotics. The oral cavity is treated with a topical antibacterial medication, such as Betadine, chlorhexidine, hydrogen peroxide, or Silvadene. Atropine injections are given if the mucus is thick; vitamin injections are given routinely, as many iguanas are on a vitamin-deficient diet. Vitamin C also seems to help in many cases of mouth rot.

The prognosis of mouth rot depends upon several factors. If the animal is still eating and not lethargic, the prognosis is good. If signs are caught very early when only the pinpoint hemorrhages are seen, the chance for recovery is excellent. Those animals that are lethargic and not eating have a more guarded prognosis. Secondary problems, such as internal parasites, must also be treated. Once the animal has recovered, diet and environment are changed as needed.

Anorexia

Ball pythons may refuse to feed for a variety of reasons (see **Feeding**). Whenever I get a call about a snake that isn't eating, I ask the owner several questions. How long have you had the snake? Newly acquired pythons usually refuse to eat. How often do you handle the snake? Frequent handling, especially of recently purchased snakes, is very stressful and often causes anorexia. What is the environment like? A hide box must be provided, as well as a heat source and UV light. A proper thermal (temperature) gradient must also exist in the cage. Water should be available 24 hours a day. Is the snake shedding or pregnant? Snakes that are shedding or pregnant won't eat. Is the snake showing any signs of illness? Sick snakes don't eat. What are you feeding the snake, and how often? Many pythons won't eat mice or rats and need to be fed gerbils; snakes fed too frequently won't eat every meal offered. If everything sounds fine, we schedule a physical examination and fecal test for parasites. Only if both the exam and parasite check are negative for signs of disease do I assume the snake is healthy. Then I discuss feeding regimens with the owner to encourage the python to begin feeding.

Respiratory Infection

Most respiratory infections are caused by bacteria, but lungworms are occasionally seen as well. The python with a respiratory infection (which I always assume is pneumonia, an infection of the lungs) usually has a large amount of mucus in its mouth, often a nasal discharge, is lethargic and refuses to eat, and usually exhibits open-mouth breathing and may be wheezing. These signs are similar to mouth rot; in fact, many snakes have both problems. These pets are gravely ill, and hospitalization is essential. Hospitalized snakes are kept in a warm incubator, given fluids, and are force-fed. Cultures of the respiratory tract are taken, and a tracheal and colonic wash are performed to check for parasites. Injectable antibiotics and vitamins are given. Once the snake begins to improve, the owner can continue antibiotic injections at home.

Septicemia

Septicemia, also called toxemia, is a generalized, widespread infection, usually bacterial in origin. It can result as a direct infection of the bloodstream, or after a localized infection, such as mouth rot, spreads into the blood. Septic animals are gravely ill and require hospitalization and intensive therapy.

Septic snakes are lethargic and refuse to eat. Often these animals have pinpoint areas of hemorrhage on the mucus membranes in their mouths and on their ventral (belly) scales.

Supportive care is similar to that for snakes hospitalized for respiratory infections.

Internal Parasites

The most commonly diagnosed parasites of pythons are parasites of the gastrointestinal tract (trichomonas and amoebae) and respiratory tract (lungworms). Gastrointestinal parasites are often diagnosed on a routine fecal examination, although blood and mucus in the stool may also be seen. Lungworms are occasionally diagnosed during the annual examination; clinical signs such as open-mouth breathing and wheezing are often seen.

Treatment involves deworming with the appropriate medication administered by the veterinarian. The deworming protocol often involves two to four dewormings several weeks apart. Medication is given until the fecal examinations fail to reveal the parasites.

External Parasites

Most reptiles rarely have external parasites, unlike dogs and cats. An exception is the snake; the most common external parasite of snakes is the snake mite. Mites are tiny black bugs that live on and between the scales; they are often seen around the eyes. The mites feed on the blood of the snake; with a heavy infestation, anemia may result. The mites are also capable of spreading infections, including mouth rot. The best way to treat snake mite infestations is with a medication called ivermectin, which can be prescribed by your veterinarian. Many pet owners, attempting to save money, buy the ivermectin at the local feed store and give it themselves. This practice is extremely dangerous; ivermectin must be diluted to the proper concentration or fatalities will occur! In addition to treating the snake, the housing must also be treated. Hot soapy water will do the trick, or a dilute bleach solution (1 part bleach to 20-30 parts of water) will also work. Be sure to thoroughly rinse and dry the cage after cleaning. Bowls, artificial plants and branches, the Astroturf, and the hiding box must also be cleaned.

Ticks may occasionally be seen on snakes. Like mites, they feed on blood and can also transmit diseases between snakes. Gentle manual removal with alcohol and a pair of tweezers can solve the problem. Have your veterinarian show you the correct way to remove ticks.

Kidney Failure

As with so many pets, kidney failure can cause death in pythons. These pets are usually older; as with mammals, kidney failure is often irreversible. With dogs and cats, we can often sustain life for a period of time. With exotic pets, too often the problem is not diagnosed until it's too late. Treatment, when attempted, is with hospitalization and aggressive fluid and antibiotic therapy.

Antibiotic Toxicity

Many antibiotics commonly administered to pets and people are toxic to reptiles if given in the wrong amount or dosage frequency. This is yet another important reason to make sure your veterinarian is qualified to treat reptiles.

Salmonella

While box turtles are infamous for carrying salmonella bacteria, any reptile can harbor this organism. This bacteria can cause severe gastrointestinal disease or septicemia (blood poisoning). Many animals and people carry the bacteria without showing any clinical signs, yet shed the bacteria in their feces, which can infect others.

Prevention through proper hygiene is the best way to control the disease. Since most animals carrying salmonella are not ill, they usually require no treatment (which often fails to kill the bacteria anyway).

Dystocia

Dystocia means "difficult birth." It occasionally occurs when an egg has trouble passing through the birth canal. When a reptile cannot pass an egg, it must have medical intervention within a reasonable period of time or it will die.

In order to suspect dystocia (also called egg retention), you need to know if your pet is a male or female. Probing of the cloacal area by a veterinarian, while not always 100% accurate, is reliable. With male pets, the probe can be inserted about twice as far as in females.

If the animal is known to be female, diagnosing the condition is a bit easier. Often one or several eggs have already passed, yet the snake continues to strain as if trying to pass the remaining eggs. Signs often seen with dystocia, even if no eggs have been passed, include refusal to eat, not moving very much, and possibly a personality change (the pet may be less active or more irritable). These signs are not unique to dystocia and can be seen with many reptile diseases.

Definitive diagnosis usually requires radiographs (X-rays); unless the shells are not calcified, the eggs are readily visible.

The cause of the dystocia is often unknown. However, a poor diet, incorrect environmental temperature, and internal diseases are all contributing factors. For whatever reason, the uterus fails to expel the eggs and they get stuck. Occasionally, the eggs are too big to pass through the cloaca, and this causes the dystocia.

The objective of treatment is to relieve the dystocia and allow the snake to pass the eggs. Depending upon the severity of the case, warming the pet, administering injectable medications, or even surgery can correct the problem.

Chapter 4

The Box Turtle

The box turtle is probably the most common species of turtle kept as a pet. Until the 1970s, these turtles were easily purchased at most pet stores. However, because of the risk of a young child placing a smaller turtle in his or her mouth and contracting salmonella, a law was passed prohibiting the sale of any turtle smaller than 4 inches in diameter.

Salmonella is a bacterium often implicated in food poisoning. While the disease rarely causes anything more serious than vomiting and diarrhea in healthy adults, young

children and people with lowered immune systems can easily develop a fatal disease. Turtles are certainly not the only animal that can spread salmonella. In fact, the disease is usually caused by contact with an infected person. However, since box turtles were a common children's pet, the danger of infection was very real. Most of the turtles carried the infection asymptomatically, which meant that they were never sick. You can imagine how easily the disease, which involves contact with infected feces, could be spread if young children were placing the turtles in their mouths! Common sense and good hygiene are essential in preventing this and most other diseases. After handling any pet, its excrement, or its bedding and toys, *thoroughly wash your hands*.

Even though this chapter is about box turtles, much of the information can be applied to other species as well. Contact your veterinarian for specific information on feeding and housing if you own another species of turtle.

General Information

Most box turtles never get very large (unlike tortoises). The average adult size for box turtles is 5-7 inches in diameter, with females being slightly smaller than males. The adult size is reached at 4-6 years of age. Turtles that are not allowed to hibernate grow at a faster rate. Sexual maturity is reached at about the fifth year of life.

The anatomy of box turtles is different from other pets. The most obvious difference is the presence of a shell, or more correctly, two shells. The top, or dorsal, shell is called the carapace; the bottom, or ventral, shell is called the plastron. In general, males have a more concave plastron than females; this concavity allows for easier mating. Males are also larger than females, and are usually more colorful (having a male and female next to each other makes the comparison easier). Males also usually have a longer and thicker tail, which once again allows for easier intromission of the penis during mating. Finally, the distance between the vent or cloaca (common opening for the digestive, urinary, and reproductive tracts) is greater in males.

With proper diet and housing, turtles can live 30-40 years or longer. Unfortunately, because of owner ignorance of the correct way to feed and house turtles, most box turtles rarely make it to their second birthday.

Muscling is limited in turtles, and many bones are replaced by the protective shells (which are hinged to allow movement). The pectoral or chest muscles are well developed. Despite the obvious lack of muscling, box turtles are extremely strong. The strength, manifested by the turtle retracting into its shell when disturbed, is one of the signs to check for when purchasing a box turtle.

Box turtles lack teeth, but they do have a strong "beak," thus, box turtles can and do bite! The other weapon of the box turtle is its claws, which should be trimmed periodically (your veterinarian can show you how).

The number of rings on the shell of the turtle have nothing to do with its age.

The protective shell makes surgery difficult. Two techniques are available for performing internal surgery. One technique is where the shell is cut and then repaired following the procedure; the second technique involves making an incision in front of and through the muscles of the pelvis and hindlimbs.

Anatomical Interests

1. Turtles have no diaphragm, but rather breathe by movements of membranes enclosing their internal organs and by movements of their legs and head.
2. Turtles have a three-chambered heart.
3. Turtles have a renal portal blood system, where blood from the hindlimbs is filtered by the kidneys before reaching the general circulation.

4. Turtles excrete uric acid as their main waste product of protein metabolism.
5. Turtles have a cloaca, which is a common opening for the digestive, urinary, and genital systems.
6. The shell is covered with bony plates called scutes. Turtles usually shed their scutes in large patches, unlike snakes which usually shed in one piece. The number of scutes have nothing to do with the turtle's age. The top bony plate is the carapace, and the bottom plate (shell) is the plastron.
7. Unlike most other reptiles, turtles have a urinary bladder.

Selecting Your Pet

Most owners buy their turtles locally from a pet store, although mail ordering from reptile breeders is also common. If you buy a pet through the mail, make sure you know what you're getting! Ask about a guarantee if the pet isn't what you want.

Ideally, you should acquire a young captive-raised animal. Older imported animals are harder to tame, may harbor internal parasites, and often suffer from the stress of captivity. Avoid sick-looking animals. Don't try to be a "Good Samaritan." Remember that with sick exotic pets, if it looks sick it's really dying! Trying to nurse a sick turtle back to health after purchasing it will rarely work. Just the stress of a new environment is often enough to kill a sick turtle.

Start out right with a healthy pet. Avoid turtles that appear skinny, have loose skin or sunken eyes, and appear inactive or lethargic. A healthy turtle is active, alert, and resists having its head and limbs extended. (Be careful not to hurt the turtle or get bitten when handling it; if the turtle retracts its head and limbs on its own, this is a sufficient show of strength.) The vent or cloaca should be clean and free of wetness or stool. *Gently* open the mouth (a paper clip works well, but be gentle; often the turtle will open its mouth as an aggressive display, enabling you to get a quick peek). There should be a small amount of clear saliva present and a dark blue or purple tongue and oral cavity. Mucus that is cloudy or has a "cottage cheese" appearance is a sign of mouth rot, as are redness or pinpoint hemorrhages on the mucus membranes. The eyes should be open and clear; eyes that are sunken into the head or swollen shut often indicate dehydration, emaciation, starvation, and vitamin A deficiency. Make sure no lumps or bumps are present on the shell or limbs; make sure the shell is clean and isn't cracked or missing scutes (plates), and that there is no sign of infection (often seen as shell discoloration or moldy growth). Of course, your new pet should be examined by a reptile veterinarian within 48 hours of purchase, so if you can't examine the mouth, he can. Even with pet stores, always inquire about the guarantee in case the turtle is found to be unhealthy.

The First Veterinary Visit

Your turtle's first veterinary visit should include determining the animal's weight, as well as checking for lumps and bumps. The turtle is examined for signs of dehydration and starvation. A fecal test is done to check for internal parasites. The oral cavity is examined for signs of infectious stomatitis (mouth rot). No vaccines are required for box turtles. Most of the visit will probably be a question-and-answer session. We spend an average of 30 minutes with all new owners of exotic pets, and give them a handout as well as suggest several good books to read. If all turns out well, your turtle will be given a clean bill of health. Like all pets, turtles should be examined and have their stool tested for parasites annually.

Housing

Box turtles may be housed inside or outside, depending upon environmental conditions and owner preference.

Indoor Housing

Most owners house their turtles in 10- or 20-gallon aquariums, which are usually adequate for indoor housing.

Substrate, or cage lining material, should be easy to clean and nontoxic to the turtle. Newspaper, butcher paper, towels, or Astroturf are recommended. Astroturf is preferred by many reptile owners. Acquire two pieces of turf and cut them to fit the bottom of the cage. With two pieces, one is always in the cage and one is kept outside the cage and is always clean. When the turf inside the cage becomes soiled, you'll always have a clean, dry piece to replace it. Clean the soiled turf with ordinary soap and water (avoid harsher products unless your reptile veterinarian OKs them), thoroughly rinse it, and hang it to dry so it will be ready for the next cage cleaning.

Avoid sand, gravel, wood shavings, corn cob material, walnut shells, and cat litter, as these are not only difficult to clean but can cause impactions if eaten on purpose or accidentally should the food become covered by these substrates. Cedar wood shavings are toxic to reptiles!

Rocks (large ones) in the cage allow for basking. A hiding place is appreciated by all reptiles and should be available. Artificial plants can be arranged to provide a hiding place, as can clay pots, cardboard boxes, and other containers that provide a secure area.

A heat source is necessary for all reptiles, which are cold-blooded and need a variety of temperatures to regulate their internal body temperature. Ideally, the cage should be set up so that a heat gradient is established, with one end warmer than the other end. In this way, the turtle can move around in its environment and warm or cool itself as needed. In order to establish and maintain the proper temperature gradient, owners should purchase two thermometers and place one at the cooler end of the cage and one at the warmer end. The cooler end of the cage should be 70-75 degrees Fahrenheit, while the warmer end should be 80-85 degrees. A convenient, inexpensive, and safe way to do this is to supply a focal heat source. A 100-watt incandescent bulb with a reflector hood works well. This heat source should be placed *outside* and above one end of the cage, which should be covered by a screen top to prevent the turtle from escaping or burning itself on the bulb. At night, heat isn't necessary as long as the temperature remains at 65-70 degrees.

A popular form of offering heat for reptiles is the infamous "Hot Rock" or "Sizzle Rock." These devices are dangerous and should be avoided! There are several reasons for this warning. With the exception of very small reptiles, they will not supply enough heat for the pet. Even if one can find a large enough rock, it is hard to find one that is safe. There are many stories of turtles burning themselves, often severely, from prolonged contact with this (and other) heat sources. Why an animal would not remove itself from a dangerously hot appliance is unknown, but it is not uncommon for reptiles to sustain severe, even fatal, burns from a Hot Rock (or an exposed 100-watt bulb). Therefore, the Hot Rocks and similar devices are not recommended!

Heating pads can be used underneath the cage, at one end of the enclosure. Two words of advice: first, make sure the pad adequately warms that part of the cage. Second, make sure it doesn't overheat the cage or you'll have a greenhouse effect. Many experts recommend elevating the cage about 1 inch off the ground with blocks and then sliding the heating pad underneath the cage. If heating pads are used, the top of the cage must not be opened (it should be covered) or too much heat will be lost. Instead, a few small holes can be cut at the top and along the lower part of the cage for ventilation and thermoregulation.

Heating tape or coils of the variety used to warm the soil for plant protection are another possibility. However, these need to be buried in the soil (which really isn't recommended as a cage substrate) and can cause harm if exposed.

Finally, room space heaters can be used if the room cools down too much at night. They probably shouldn't be the only heat source, as they don't allow for a cooler area of the cage.

A source of vitamin D also must be provided. As discussed below, lack of vitamin D is a major cause of metabolic bone disease. While vitamin D certainly should be provided in the diet, it is still necessary to provide it to the turtle by using UV light. In addition to providing vitamin D, these lights, as well as full spectrum lights, also seem to have a positive impact on the psychological well-being of the pet.

The best recommendation is to provide light and UV light using a two-bulb fixture. Ideally, the UV light should emit light in the UV-B range (290-320 nanometers). Combining a black light (such as one from General Electric) with a Vita-Lite, Chroma-50, or Colortone-50 in a two-bulb fixture seems to meet the needs of the turtle. Other acceptable UV lights include the TL-09 and TL-12 from Philips, and the Ultra-Vitalux from Osram. The plant black light from Sylvania, the Gro-Lux, definitely needs to be combined with a UV light. The UV output of these lights decreases with age; many recommend replacing the lights at least yearly, and some (including myself) suggest every six months. For UV light to work, it must reach the pet in an unfiltered form, which means that you must make sure there is no glass or plastic interposed between the pet and the light.

Plant lights (without additional UV light supplementation) and poster-type black lights are not recommended, as they don't provide much light in the required 290-320 nanometer range.

Exposing the turtle to direct, unfiltered sunlight is always a good idea, as the UV portion of sunlight is filtered by plastic or glass. Several words of caution should be mentioned. First, putting a glass aquarium in direct sunlight can easily cause the aquarium to get dangerously hot (similar to leaving a child or pet in a closed car in the summer). Second, taking the pet out of its normal cage is fine, but care must be taken to prevent its escape or attack by other pets. An outdoor cage constructed of wood and wire screen is an acceptable method of exposing reptiles to sunlight. Finally, some reptiles become aggressive immediately following exposure to sunlight. Care should be used when handling reptiles immediately after a "sunbath."

Outdoor Housing

Many turtles do well outdoors in the warmer months. For their own protection, they should be kept within an enclosure. Make sure a shaded area is provided, as well as a hiding area. Turtles can dig out of enclosures, so make sure to bury the fencing 6-12 inches or put bricks or rocks under the area. Some owners find a children's wading pool a suitable environment. Astroturf can be used for lining material, or grass, twigs, and other natural material will be fine if it is changed daily (avoid cedar as it is toxic to reptiles). Of course, food and fresh water must always be available. Bring the turtle indoors if the temperature drops below 60 degrees. Finally, remember that turtles can become prey for neighborhood dogs and cats, so keep this in mind when housing a turtle outdoors.

The turtle should receive about twelve hours of light and twelve hours of darkness each day. Make sure the cage or room is warm enough when the lights are turned out. Infrared heat lamps can be used outside of the cage during the dark periods if needed.

Common sense dictates that fresh water be available at all times.

Finally, turtles appreciate a "private" area where they can hide. A clay pot or shoe box usually works well.

Hibernation

If given the opportunity, turtles will hibernate. It is not necessary that they hibernate, but some owners wish to provide suitable conditions for hibernating. Hibernation is necessary for adequate reproduction. If the temperature of the environment stays warm, some turtles may stop eating in the fall, but many will continue feeding and skip hibernation. Hibernation is very stressful, and subclinical illnesses can manifest themselves during hibernation. *Only turtles that are in good health should be allowed to hibernate, so a thorough examination and appropriate laboratory tests are essential prior to hibernation!*

If you elect to allow hibernation, it usually begins in the fall (September or October). Often as the temperature drops, especially if the cage temperature cools, the turtle's appetite will decrease. At this time, withhold food but not water for 1-2 weeks and keep the temperature at 70-80 degrees. This will allow the turtle the chance to eliminate and clear its gastrointestinal tract. After this period, remove the external heat source for a week and allow the turtle to remain at room temperature (60-70 degrees). Then, the turtle can be placed in its hibernating compartment (hibernaculum).

The hibernaculum should have dim light and the temperature should be between 50-60 degrees. An occasional drop to 45 degrees is OK. Persistent temperatures above 60 degrees are not cool enough for true hibernation and allow the turtle's metabolism to increase, causing it to slowly starve. (I call this "pseudohibernation," and it is a common but unfortunate occurrence.) Temperatures below 45 degrees are detrimental as well. For the safety of the turtle, it should not be allowed to hibernate outdoors as temperature and predators can't be controlled.

The hibernaculum should have a foot of humid peat-based potting soil and a 3- to 6-inch layer of shredded newspaper or leaves or hay on top, allowing the turtle to burrow. The soil should remain damp but not wet to prevent the turtle from dehydrating. A small water bowl should be present to offer humidity and prevent dehydration. As a rule, turtles will hibernate for 3 to 5 months. Any turtle that appears ill during hibernation (check your turtle at least weekly) should be immediately seen by your veterinarian. Pneumonia is often seen during hibernation; signs of this disease include nasal discharge, mucus in the mouth, and gurgling respiratory noises.

At the end of hibernation (early spring), the turtle should be placed back in its regular cage and the temperature slowly warmed to the normal range over a one-week period; food should then be offered.

Feeding

There is currently much misinformation concerning the feeding of exotic pets presented in books available for purchase by the public. These books encourage turtle owners to feed their pets only insects, insects and fruit, insects and fruit cocktail, dog food, and cat food. Improper feeding is *the* major cause of many diseases seen in box turtles. If nothing else, my intention in writing this book is for owners of exotic pets to provide their pets the proper diet and environment. Doing just these two things will prevent most of the diseases commonly seen.

In the wild, box turtles are omnivorous, meaning they eat both plant and animal matter. This makes them relatively easy to feed. Variety is the key. Make sure the food is chopped into small pieces so the turtle can eat it.

As a rule, 50% of the diet can be plant-based matter and 50% can be animal-based matter. Of the plant matter, most (80%) should be vegetable- or flower-based, and only 20% fruit based. Even though turtles enjoy the sweetness of fruit, compared to vegetables fruits are usually vitamin- and mineral-deficient. Consider fruit as mainly a treat.

As a rule, anything green and leafy should make up a large part of the diet. Yellow and orange vegetables should also be included. Avoid fiber-rich, vitamin-deficient vegetables including lettuce and celery; their composition is mainly fiber and water with little nutritional vaule.

Acceptable vegetables include collard greens, mustard greens, turnip greens, alfalfa hay or chow, bok choy, kale, parsley, spinach (in small amounts), bell pepper, green beans, green peas, corn, okra, cactus, various squashes, sweet potatoes, cabbage or broccoli (also in small amounts), and flowers such as carnations, hibiscus, and roses (avoid azaleas as they are toxic). Many turtles will also eat grass and hay, such as alfalfa hay. Make sure the hay or grass has not recently been treated for pests or fertilized!

Vegetables can be offered cooked or raw (thoroughly wash raw veggies); experiment with your turtle to see if he prefers his vegetables raw or cooked. Flowers can be homegrown or purchased from floral shops. Often, floral shops throw out older, wilting flowers. Since these may be unacceptable for sale to the public, reptile owners can often get them free. Make sure that no chemicals have been applied to the flowers or water.

Fruit can include apples, pears, bananas, grapes, peaches, kiwis, and melons. Fruits that are particularly healthy include figs (which contain calcium), papaya, raspberries, and strawberries.

Appropriate protein sources include crickets, sardines (drained), tofu, hard-boiled eggs, earthworms, and mealworms. Dog food and cat food contain too much vitamin D and fat and should not be fed. Reptile pellets, bird pellets, trout chow, and other fish chows are excellent protein sources; feeding these precludes the need for live prey (although you can feed live prey as well, as turtles often enjoy the psychological stimulation of catching the live prey).

Live prey, such as crickets and worms, either should be raised by the owner or purchased from a pet store or reptile breeder. *Never* feed your turtle insects taken from the family garden. Raising your own insects is easy; the Chicago Herpetological Society has an excellent manual entitled

The Right Way to Feed Insect-Eating Lizards discussing this topic. If you get your insects from a local pet store, it is a good idea to "nutrient load" them prior to feeding them to your turtle. Keep them in a container and feed the insects finely ground rodent chow or fish chow. Fish flakes blended with calcium carbonate powder and high protein baby cereal flakes can also be fed to the insects. A slice of orange (for crickets) or sweet potato (for mealworms) can serve as a water source for the insects. Insects should be fed at least a few days before offering them to your turtle. Prior to feeding your turtle, lightly sprinkle the insects with a good multivitamin powder (available at pet stores or from your veterinarian).

It is recommended by many veterinarians to *lightly* sprinkle all the food offered to the turtle with a calcium powder (calcium gluconate, lactate, or carbonate). Weekly, a light sprinkling of a good reptile vitamin on the food is also recommended. A light dusting means just that; oversupplementation can cause problems. Think of a light sprinkling the same way you would lightly salt food for yourself!

Juvenile turtles should be fed daily, while adults can be fed daily or every other day. These are just guidelines, as many adults will eat daily.

Fresh water in a crock that won't easily tip over should be available at all times. Turtles will not only drink from the water bowl but will often bathe in it as well (although it is perfectly acceptable to mist the turtle with water a few times a week too). Make sure the water stays clean; many reptiles love to eliminate in their water bowl as well as drink from it.

In summary, variety is the key. Don't let your turtle get "hooked" on just one or two favorite items. Feed many items in small portions. Make sure the food is the right size for your pet: smaller animals need their food finely chopped. As with all pets, fresh vegetables and fruits are preferred, frozen is second best, and canned is least desirable. Make up about a week's worth and refrigerate or freeze the remaining portions for your convenience. Remember, your pet is what it eats, and when feeding insects, your pet is what its prey eats, so feed the prey properly, too!

Common Diseases

As with most exotic pets, the most common turtle diseases occur as a result of owner misinformation. Improper feeding and improper environment (housing) contribute to most of the problems seen by reptile veterinarians. Even many infections are secondary to poor environment and diet. Therefore, with proper knowledge, some of the diseases frequently seen in turtles can be prevented.

Metabolic Bone Disease

This disease is also called nutritional osteodystrophy and nutritional secondary hyperparathyroidism. The condition results from a lack of calcium and/or vitamin D in the diet.

Calcium is needed for many things in a pet's body. The correct levels of calcium need to be maintained in the bloodstream; otherwise, seizures and cardiac arrest may occur. The body has several intricate physiological mechanisms to maintain a normal level of calcium in the blood. Dietary calcium is absorbed by the intestines under the influence of vitamin D, which can be obtained through the diet or through UV light (including sunlight). Calcium is stored in the bones under the influence of a hormone called calcitonin. When the blood calcium level decreases, several things happen: the kidneys excrete less calcium in the urine, more calcium is absorbed by the intestines, and calcium is removed from the bones under the influence of another hormone called parathyroid hormone.

When the diet contains inadequate amounts of calcium or vitamin D, over a period of time too much calcium is taken from the bones. The result is a bone with a thin outer layer (cortex) which is very prone to fracturing (breaking). While all bones in the body can be affected, early signs are usually seen in the lower jawbone, or mandible, which becomes rubbery and pliable (a slang term for this disease is "rubber jaw"). Even though the blood calcium level usually remains normal, the animal can show signs of illness. The most commonly seen signs include weakness, lethargy, and anorexia (refusal to eat).

Turtles with metabolic bone disease often have swellings of the jaws or in rare cases the legs. This swollen tissue is actually fibrous connective tissue that forms as a consequence of this disease. Often shell deformities such as a curved rim of the shell are also seen.

If this is a result of an improper diet or environment, what foods are the most common offending items? Well, meat is known to contain very little calcium. Any animal or person fed a diet composed entirely of meat is going to develop metabolic bone disease. Box turtles maintained entirely on crickets and fruit cocktail (unfortunately a common scenario) also are eating a calcium-deficient diet. Most of these pets are usually not receiving any mineral or vitamin supplementation, or any UV light. You can easily see how this disease can either be prevented or caused by the owner.

Clinical signs of metabolic bone disease include swelling and flexibility of the mandible (lower jaw). While this is the earliest sign of this disease, most owners don't detect the problem at this stage. Typically, the pet isn't brought in for a checkup until it becomes lethargic, stops eating, and can't move. In my experience, if the pet is still eating and somewhat active, the chance for a cure is much better.

A complete examination is needed. Often, these animals also have mouth rot and are infected with internal parasites. A good exam and radiographs (X-rays) can provide a lot of information. The rule in medicine is to "treat the pet, not the disease." Therefore, individuals with parasites, mouth rot, or other problems need these addressed as well as the metabolic bone disease.

Turtles that are still active and eating can be treated at home. Injections of calcium gluconate are given by the owner in the pet's peritoneal (abdominal) cavity; most owners can be easily taught this procedure. A UV light is supplied as well. Often, a vitamin injection is also given. I try not to correct the improper diet until the animal has recovered from the diseases; then, the diet is slowly changed. Recovery, if it occurs, should be seen after 4-6 weeks of injections. Owners are instructed to remove all objects from the cage except the food and water bowls. The bones and shells of these sick pets are very fragile and can easily fracture if the turtle falls off a basking area or a branch falls onto the pet.

Turtles that are lethargic and not eating always have a guarded prognosis, but treatment should always be attempted. I advise owners that while many pets that are severely ill will die, about 20% won't, and since we can't tell which category any pet falls into, we should attempt treatment. These animals are very sick and need to be hospitalized. They are placed in an incubator and given intraperitoneal fluids. We also force-feed them in an attempt to get them to start eating. If improvement is to be seen, it usually occurs within three days of intensive care.

After the disease is cured, the owners are shown how to slowly correct the diet; UV light and vitamins and minerals are provided as well.

Hypovitaminosis A

A deficiency of vitamin A is commonly seen in box turtles that are fed improperly. The all-meat diet or the "cricket and fruit cocktail" diet or the "lettuce and carrots" diet, are all deficient in vitamin A. Vitamin A is needed to maintain intact epithelium. Lack of this vitamin produces signs seen with changes in the epidermis (outer layer of skin and mucus membranes). The turtle may show a lack of appetite, lethargy, swelling of the eyes and eyelids (often with a pus-type discharge), swelling of the ears (actually an ear abscess), and respiratory infection.

Diagnosis is easily made by the clinical signs and nutritional history.

Treatment includes correcting the diet and supplying vitamin A. Hospitalization is also needed for severe cases that require incubation, fluid therapy, antibiotics for secondary infections, and force-feeding to correct the high calcium level. Injectable vitamin A can be used, but it is easy to cause another problem, hypervitaminosis A, due to vitamin A overdose. While there is nothing wrong with injectable Vitamin A, many veterinarians choose to correct the problem with oral vitamin A. Prevention is once again the best medicine.

Infectious Stomatitis

This condition is more commonly known by the term "mouth rot." The disease is almost always caused by bacteria. While many bacteria are capable of causing the problem, Pseudomonas and Aeromonas are the most common. Many doctors feel that this disease is always a secondary one, which means something must set it off. These doctors feel this way because Pseudomonas and Aeromonas bacteria are often normally present in a reptile's environment and body. Certainly a filthy environment is a common cause of this disease. Other stressors that can cause the disease include internal parasites, poor diet, improper environment and improper environmental temperature (low body temperature in any animal decreases the ability of the body's immune system to fight off infection), shipping (as when a pet is purchased and brought into the owner's home), too little or too much handling, a too humid or too dry environment, and almost any other type of stress! The stress is not always identified, but the pet should undergo a thorough diagnostic workup. (Treat the pet, not the disease!)

Early signs that often go unnoticed by owners are small, pinpoint areas of hemorrhage inside the oral cavity (roof or floor of the mouth and gums). The later stages of the disease reveal a large amount of frothy, bubbly mucus or a cottage cheese-type material in the mouth. Many animals in these later stages are anorectic (not eating) and lethargic.

Diagnosis is fairly easy and is made by observation of the oral cavity. All cases and suspected cases of mouth rot should be cultured. Pseudomonas and Aeromonas are found in many normal reptiles, so just finding them on a culture doesn't always means the pet has or will develop mouth rot. However, any heavy growth of either bacteria on a culture should probably be treated.

A culture gives several pieces of advice. First, it confirms whether or not bacteria or fungi are seen in the mucus. (This is especially helpful in "borderline" cases, where the doctor feels the amount of mucus in the mouth is abnormal but isn't quite sure if it's necessarily anything to worry about.) Second, the culture tells us specifically which bacteria or fungus is present and causing the disease. Finally, the culture tells us which drug (antibiotic) should be used to treat the infection.

Treatment varies with the severity of the illness. As with many diseases, pets that are not eating and are lethargic need hospitalization. During hospitalization, these animals are given fluids (to prevent dehydration as well as to prevent toxic levels of antibiotics from damaging the kidneys), kept warm in an incubator, and force-fed. (All sick animals need to be fed to prevent the harmful effects seen with anorexia, such as muscle wasting and depressed immune systems.)

While awaiting the culture results, the turtles are started on injectable antibiotics. The oral cavity is treated with a topical antibacterial medication, such as Betadine, chlorhexidine, hydrogen peroxide, or Silvadene. Atropine injections are given if the mucus is thick; vitamin injections are given routinely, as many turtles are on a vitamin-deficient diet. Vitamin C also seems to help in many cases of mouth rot.

The prognosis of mouth rot depends upon several factors. If the animal is still eating and not lethargic, the prognosis is good. If signs are caught very early when only the pinpoint hemorrhages are seen, the chance for recovery is excellent. Those animals that are lethargic and not eating have a more guarded prognosis. Secondary problems, such as internal parasites, must also be treated. Once the animal has recovered, diet and environment are changed as needed.

Respiratory Infections

Most respiratory infections are caused by bacteria, and in turtles they are often secondary to vitamin A deficiency and mouth rot. The turtle with a respiratory infection (which I always assume is pneumonia, an infection of the lungs) usually has a large amount of mucus in its mouth, often a nasal discharge, is lethargic and refuses to eat, and usually exhibits open-mouth breathing and may be wheezing. These signs are similar to mouth rot; in fact, many turtles have both problems. These pets are gravely ill and hospitalization is essential. Hospitalized turtles are kept in a warm incubator, given warm-water baths, and given fluids and force-fed. Cultures of the respiratory tract are taken, and a tracheal and colonic wash are performed to check for parasites. Injectable antibiotics and vitamins are given. Once the turtle begins to improve, the owner can continue antibiotic injections at home.

Abscesses

Unlike mammals, birds and reptiles usually don't form liquid pus. When these pets form abscesses, they appear as hard lumps (like tumors). This makes it difficult if not impossible to diagnose an abscess, as an aspirate of the lump is usually unrewarding (in mammals, an aspirate usually reveals liquid pus). Diagnosis and treatment are the same, namely opening the abscess under anesthesia, cleaning it out, and using antibiotics based on culturing the material in the abscess. Abscesses in turtles are often related to vitamin A deficiency.

Cystic Calculi

Commonly called bladder stones, these occur when minerals from the diet form crystals which then form stones. Usually these are composed of uric acid, which usually results from a diet that contains too much protein.

Blood in the droppings can be seen, as well as abdominal swelling. An examination and radiographs allow the diagnosis to be confirmed. Surgical removal of the stone is needed, as is fluid therapy to prevent kidney damage; the diet should be corrected if possible to prevent future stones from forming.

Parasites

Reptiles get "worms" just like dogs and cats. Even captive-bred animals can become infected with intestinal parasites. Roundworms seem particularly common in box turtles. An annual stool exam is needed to make sure the pet remains free of parasites.

Kidney Failure

As with so many pets, kidney failure can cause death in turtles. These pets are usually older, and often the kidney failure is due to the same high-protein diet that causes bladder stones. As with mammals, kidney failure is often irreversible. With dogs and cats, we can often sustain life for a period of time. With exotic pets, too often the problem is not diagnosed until it's too late. Treatment, when attempted, is with hospitalization and aggressive fluid and antibiotic therapy.

Antibiotic Toxicity

Many antibiotics commonly used in pets and people are toxic to reptiles if given in the wrong amount or dosage frequency. This is yet another important reason to make sure your veterinarian is qualified to treat reptiles.

Salmonella

As stated in the beginning of this chapter, box turtles are infamous for carrying salmonella bacteria. This bacteria can cause severe gastrointestinal disease or septicemia (blood poisoning). Many animals and people carry the bacteria without showing any clinical signs, yet shed the bacteria in their feces which can infect others.

Again, prevention through proper hygiene is the best way to control the disease. Since most animals that carry salmonella are not ill, they usually require no treatment (which often fails to kill the bacteria anyway).

Dystocia

Dystocia means "difficult birth." It occasionally occurs when an egg has trouble passing through the birth canal. When a reptile cannot pass an egg, it must have medical intervention within a reasonable period of time or it will die.

If the animal is known to be female, diagnosing the condition is a bit easier. Often one or several eggs have already passed, yet the turtle continues to strain as if trying to pass the remaining eggs. Signs often seen with dystocia, even if no eggs have been passed, include refusal to eat, not moving very much, and possibly a personality change (the pet may be less active or more irritable). These signs are not unique to dystocia and can be seen with many reptile diseases.

Definitive diagnosis usually requires radiographs (X-rays); unless the shells are not calcified, the eggs are readily visible.

The cause of the dystocia is often unknown. However, a poor diet, incorrect environmental temperature, and internal diseases are all contributing factors. For whatever reason, the uterus fails to expel the eggs and they get stuck. Occasionally, the eggs are too big to pass through the cloaca, and this causes the dystocia.

The objective of treatment is to relieve the dystocia and allow the turtle to pass the eggs. Depending upon the severity of the case, warming the pet, administering injectable medications, or even surgery can correct the problem.

Chapter 5

The Ferret

General Information

Ferrets come in several different color combinations: the fitch ferret is the most popular. Fitch ferrets have a buff-colored coat with black markings on the face, feet, and tail. Albino ferrets are white with pink eyes. Some ferrets have a buff coat with light markings.

The female is called a jill, the male is a hob, and the infants are called kits.

The gestation period, or length of pregnancy, is about 42 days (compared to 60 days for dogs and cats and 270 days for people). Like puppies and kittens, kits are born deaf and with their eyes closed. They begin walking by about 3 weeks of age, which is also when their eyes and ears open. By about 6 weeks of age, they can be weaned onto kitten or ferret food. The average life span is 5-8 years; ferrets are considered geriatric pets at 3 years of age (compared to 8 years of age for dogs and cats).

Ferrets can make good pets. Their diet is cat food or ferret food, and they easily learn to use a litterbox. *They can be nippy and are not recommended for families with small children.*

Ferrets are escape artists and are easily able to squeeze through the tiniest openings and cracks. Homes must be "ferret-proofed" to prevent escape and injury. Naturally inquisitive, they will chew on and swallow many things. Treat your ferret like you would an infant, and always try to prevent problems. It is highly recommended to put a collar with a bell attached on your ferret so that it can be found easily if it escapes your sight (make sure the bell can't be swallowed if it becomes detached, or make sure it's firmly secured to the collar and can't easily detach). Try not to let your ferret out of your sight when it's out of its cage. If you leave the room even for a minute, take the ferret with you or put it back in its cage (carrier).

As ferrets love to chew, rubber toys are not safe for them; they often chew off and swallow small pieces. Diagnosis of an obstruction is often difficult in a ferret; usually the problem is diagnosed during exploratory surgery and is often fatal if not treated early. Hard toys like Nylabones are safe, as are rawhide treats in small amounts (although some veterinarians feel rawhide shouldn't be given to any pets). Other safe toys include ping pong and golf balls, small cans, cardboard mailing tubes, and very hard plastic toys. Cloth toys are OK if the ferret is not chewing off pieces of it!

Ferrets are usually spayed or neutered and descented prior to purchase. Unless you want to breed your prospective pet, sterilization is preferred. Intact (unneutered) male ferrets have a musky odor and can be aggressive; female ferrets never go out of heat unless bred. This prolonged heat results in bone marrow suppression from high levels of estrogen, which is fatal unless treated early and aggressively with blood transfusions.

The anal sacs of ferrets secrete a foul-smelling liquid, and thus descented ferrets (which have these sacs removed at the time of spaying and neutering) make better pets. Even after descenting, ferrets still have a slightly musky odor. Bathing can be done weekly or every other week with a gentle moisturizing shampoo that your veterinarian recommends.

Ferrets should also have their sharp claws trimmed regularly (ask your veterinarian for instructions). Ferrets should not be declawed.

Similarity to Cats

As a rule, anything that's safe for cats is safe for ferrets. This includes shampoos, food, and most medications (check with your veterinarian before using *any* medication).

Vaccinations

Just like dogs and cats, ferrets require a series of vaccinations as youngsters. Once a year, they also require an examination, a fecal test for internal parasites, and vaccination boosters. Once a ferret becomes 3 years of age, it requires a complete geriatric profile (see below).

Ferrets are usually vaccinated at 8, 12, and 16 weeks of age against canine distemper. There is an approved vaccine for rabies in ferrets. However, since many state laws vary regarding ferret bites, some veterinarians (including myself) do not vaccinate ferrets for rabies.

Anatomical Interests

1. Ferrets do not have any identifiable blood types; if needed, blood from a dog or preferably a cat can be given to a ferret that needs a blood transfusion.
2. Ferrets are very susceptible to hypoglycemia (low blood sugar). For this reason, they are only fasted for a few hours (rather than overnight) prior to surgery or blood sampling.
3. Ferrets, like many small mammals and pocket pets, are extremely susceptible to heat stress or stroke. The temperature must be kept below 90 degrees.

Selecting Your Pet

Some areas make it illegal to own a pet ferret, due to potential attacks on people and the chance of an escaped ferret becoming established in the wild (and potentially destroying crops). If owning a ferret is legal in your area, you can purchase one at a pet store or through breeders or ferret club members. Look for a young ferret (ideally). The eyes and nose should be clear and free of any discharge that might indicate a respiratory infection (or distemper). The ferret should be curious and inquisitive; it should not be thin and emaciated. Check for the presence of wetness around the anus, which might indicate diarrhea. Check for the presence of external parasites such as fleas. If possible, examine the ferret's mouth for broken teeth, discolored gums (they should be light pink), or any obvious sores, any of which could suggest disease. Inquire as to whether the ferret has been surgically altered (spayed or neutered) or descented (had its anal sacs surgically removed); these operations are usually performed by 8-12 weeks of age.

The First Veterinary Visit

Your ferret should be examined by a veterinarian within 48 hours of purchase (this is often required by the seller or the guarantee is voided). The doctor will discuss proper diet, housing, and toys for the ferret. A vaccination program will be set up, a fecal sample checked for worms, and the ferret will usually be started on heartworm preventative. Go with a list of questions, and you'll start off on the right track. Ferrets require annual veterinary visits.

Once a ferret reaches 3 years of age, a complete geriatric workup, which includes an EKG, urinalysis, blood profile, and radiographs (X-rays), is necessary for the early detection of diseases so commonly seen in older ferrets, such as cardiomyopathy and cancer.

Housing

Due to their reputation as curious creatures and escape artists, ferrets should be housed in a carrier that is securely closed and locked. Towels can be used for bedding. Ferrets like to burrow, so the towels can serve this purpose or a container such as a shoebox can be placed in the cage. A litterbox can be placed in the cage for elimination.

Diet

Ferrets eat cat food or ferret food; pet vitamins can be offered as you would for dogs and cats. Fresh water in sturdy crocks or bowls should be available at all times.

Diseases

Aplastic Anemia

Aplastic anemia literally refers to bone marrow suppression, which results in a complete loss of red blood cells (and often white blood cells and platelets) in the bone marrow.

This disease is rarely seen due to early (prepurchase) spaying of female ferrets.

The anemia occurs in intact (unspayed) ferrets that are not bred when they enter their heat cycles. Unlike most mammals, ferrets must be bred when in heat in order for them to come out of heat. Otherwise, they stay in heat indefinitely. While in heat, the ferret's estrogen levels remain high. High doses of estrogen are very toxic to bone marrow.

Signs of aplastic anemia include lethargy and pale mucus membranes in a female intact ferret that is obviously in heat (manifested by a swollen vulva, the outer lips of the female reproductive tract).

Treatment includes hormonal therapy to bring the ferret out of heat, antibiotics, iron, vitamins, and often blood transfusions. After stabilization, the ferret is spayed. Ferrets with extremely low packed cell volumes, which measure the red blood cell mass, usually are beyond help and euthanasia is recommended. This is a very serious and often expensive disease to treat. All female ferrets that will not be bred at every heat cycle should be spayed by 4-6 months of age.

Heat Stroke

Ferrets are very susceptible to extreme heat, and as such their environmental temperature should be kept below 90 degrees. Just like dogs and cats, ferrets don't sweat. Heat stroke is manifested by open mouth breathing and an elevated rectal temperature (normal temperature is 100-104; average temperature is about the same as dog and cats (101.5)). Heat stroke is a true emergency. First aid involves rapidly cooling the ferret by running cold water over its body, fanning it, or whatever is needed to rapidly reduce its body temperature. Be careful not to chill the ferret or cause shivering; if shivering results, stop the cooling process. After a few minutes of attempted cooling, rush the ferret to your veterinarian. Medical care by your veterinarian includes temperature reduction (often with cold water enemas or cold fluids instilled into its abdominal cavity). Hospitalization is required to monitor vital signs.

Canine Distemper

Ferrets can contract the dog distemper virus, which, in both, is fatal (100% in ferrets, almost 100% in dogs). Ferrets should be vaccinated against this disease. Clinical signs include loss of appetite, a thick eye and/or nasal discharge (similar to pus), and often a rash on the chin, abdomen, or groin. Treatment is supportive and should be attempted, as the disease mimics human influenza. The difference is that with distemper, the ferret will be dead within 1-2 weeks, whereas with influenza the ferret should be better within 1-2 weeks.

Human Influenza

Ferrets can contract and spread human influenza, or flu. Signs are similar to flu in humans (or to ferrets with distemper). Treatment consists of antibiotics and decongestants. Occasionally fluid therapy or force-feeding by the veterinarian will need to be done. *Never* give your ferret any over-the-counter medications or prescription drugs without checking with the doctor first. Like dogs and cats, ferrets can be easily poisoned or killed with common human medications!

Parasites

Like dogs and cats, ferrets can contract "worms." Yearly stool checks will allow easy diagnosis and treatment. External parasites, such as fleas, ticks, mange, and ear mites, can also infest ferrets. Treatment by the veterinarian is similar to treatment for dogs and cats. Owners should avoid home treatment without a proper diagnosis, as many parasites appear similar and mimic each other.

Dermatomycosis (Ringworm)

This is occasionally seen in ferrets and usually manifests as a circular area of hair loss with slight scaliness along the periphery of the circle. Diagnosis can only be accurately made with a special culture of the skin, scales, and hair. It can be transmitted to other pets and to people, so care should be used in handling infected ferrets. Treatment is similar to that for dogs and cats and involves medicated shampooing, topical medications, and oral medication for severe infections. Mild infections often respond to topical therapy alone.

Heartworm Disease

Like dogs and outdoor cats, ferrets are susceptible to heartworm disease. They should be placed on the same preventative as dogs. Blood tests are less accurate than for dogs and cats, and the diagnosis is often made using other tests such as radiographs. Treatment exists for dogs but hasn't really been used extensively with ferrets, as it may be associated with severe and fatal side effects (unlike with dogs).

Cardiomyopathy

Cardiomyopathy means "sick heart." As in cats, primary heart disease is common in ferrets. Basically, in cardiomyopathy the heart enlarges and is unable to pump blood adequately to maintain oxygen supply to the vital organs. Fluid can build up in the lungs (edema). Weakness, lethargy, and lack of appetite are often seen, as is difficulty with breathing. Cardiomyopathy is yet another disease that can present the very typical "chronic wasting" signs seen so commonly with many ferret diseases.

Diagnosis is usually made easily on physical examination; radiographs and EKGs confirm the severity of the problem. A special test, cardiac ultrasound, is also used to determine the ability of the heart to pump blood and to determine the type of heart failure present (a dilated, thin-walled heart, or a thickened heart).

Treatment involves diuretic drugs to remove fluid from the lungs, as well as drugs to strengthen the heart and reduce the pressure buildup in the veins and arteries to make it easier for the heart to pump blood. Oxygen is used in emergency situations to stabilize the ferret.

Cancer

Unfortunately, ferrets contract cancer quite readily and quite early in life. Since early detection is critical to survival, *every ferret three years of age and older should have a geriatric screening at least annually (and preferably every six months)*. This screening includes a complete blood count and organ profile, radiographs (X-rays) of the chest and abdomen, urinalysis, and an EKG.

There are several types of cancers commonly seen in the pet ferret. Cancer of the pancreas is common and is called insulinoma. This tumor secretes a large supply of insulin, which causes the ferret's blood glucose (blood sugar) to fall to dangerously low levels. As with so many diseases, signs are subtle and weakness is commonly seen. Often, weakness of the hindquarters is seen, and sometimes excess salivation or pawing at the mouth (indicating nausea) are seen.

Diagnosis is usually easily made with a blood glucose test. Treatment is medical or surgical plus medical. If possible, tumors are removed during surgery (this is not always possible, as many small tumors might be present). This is a serious disease that must be treated aggressively.

Another type of tumor seen in geriatric ferrets is an adrenal gland tumor. This tumor is often seen in conjunction with the insulinoma. Currently, it is not possible to diagnose this disease with any laboratory tests. It is diagnosed based on clinical signs and exploratory surgery and biopsy. Signs include hair loss (usually starting at the rear end of the ferret and progressing forward), thin skin, enlarged vulva, body odor, wasting, weakness, and in rare instances increased water intake and urination. Treatment involves removal of the affected adrenal gland or glands during the exploratory surgery. Even without surgery, tumors of the adrenal gland usually progress very slowly, and many animals may live several years without treatment. Periodic blood testing is needed to check for bone marrow suppression.

A final cancer commonly seen in ferrets is lymphosarcoma, which is cancer of the lymph nodes and lymphocytic white blood cells. Early in the disease we see the same subtle signs so commonly seen in most ferret diseases, such as weakness, wasting, weight loss, and lack of appetite. More obvious signs of lymphosarcoma can be seen as the disease progresses, including lymph node swelling. Without this swelling, diagnosis is difficult from just the clinical signs and relies on checking the white blood cell count as well as the lymphocyte count of the pet. Often lymph node biopsies are recommended as well.

Chemotherapy works well in this type of cancer. Prior to treatment, it is important to screen for those other diseases so commonly seen in ferrets older than three years of age, as often more than one serious disease is present in the same pet.

Many veterinarians recommend screening ferrets with a blood count as early as one year of age to check for this disease.

Other types of cancers can occur in ferrets; any lump or bump should be immediately aspirated by your veterinarian to check for cancer. Treated early, many types of cancers can be cured.

Bladder Stones

Bladder problems develop frequently in ferrets as in cats. Stones can develop in the bladder, or crystals that don't form stones can develop (as in cats with lower urinary tract disease, or feline urological syndrome) and cause urinary tract blockage.

Signs can include excessive urination (in reality, the ferrets are urinating more often than normal but the volume of urine is usually very scant with each urinary episode), blood in the urine, straining to urinate (which indicates an obstruction of the urethra, the tube that leads from the bladder to the vulva or penis), or a consistently wet perineum (the area around the anus). Since the urethra is longer and narrower in hobs, they are more likely to have an obstruction than the jills.

Diagnosis is often made during a physical examination, as the stones are usually easy to feel in the bladder. In the case where only crystalline debris is present, the history, signs, and urinalysis are often informative.

Treatment involves dietary manipulation and often surgery as well. As with the disease in cats, ferrets are placed on a medicated diet that does two things: First, the food contains acidifying drugs to cause the urine to be acid. The type of crystals most often involved in this disease easily dissolve in acid urine. Secondly, the diet also contains restricted amounts of the minerals magnesium, calcium, and phosphorus, which are the minerals that usually form the crystals which can then form the stones. Bladder infections are treated with antibiotics.

Urinary obstruction is a life-threatening condition. In cats, the urethra is easy to flush (most of the time) while the cat is anesthetized. This is difficult in ferrets, and some veterinarians recommend bladder surgery to remove the crystalline debris. Ferrets usually tolerate the surgery quite well. Diet is changed under veterinary supervision after the disease is brought under control. Since drinking large amounts of water means frequent urination which in turn means frequent bladder flushing, fresh water should always be available in bowls, as ferrets seem to drink more from bowls than from water bottles or nipples.

Diarrhea

Diarrhea is not a disease per se, but rather a sign of a gastrointestinal problem. In ferrets, there are several conditions that can result in diarrhea. As with dogs and cats, internal parasites should be the first thing checked for. A simple stool examination under a microscope allows the veterinarian to easily diagnose internal parasites. A stool examination should be performed at the ferret's yearly checkup and vaccination visit.

Viruses can also cause diarrhea in ferrets. Ferrets can be affected by a disease often seen in mink called *Aleutian disease*, which is caused by a parvovirus. The predominant sign is chronic wasting, and often black, tarry stools are seen. Blood tests reveal an increase in the gamma globulin proteins. No treatment exists for this disease.

Rotavirus infection is a problem in 1- to 3-week-old ferrets; since most owners do not acquire their pets at this age, rotaviral infections will probably not be the cause of your ferret's diarrhea. Young ferrets may develop one of two wasting diseases that can cause diarrhea. Helicobacter musteli is a spirochete-type of bacterium. This spirochete is closely related to other Helicobacter bacteria that cause similar problems in people and other mammalian pets. Not much is known about how ferrets contract the disease, but it is felt that all ferrets probably carry Helicobacter and that some stressful event (not always identified) allows it to cause ulcers. Signs of this ulcerative disease include ferrets suddenly becoming thin and passing dark, tarry stools. Treatment is similar to that of people who have Helicobacter ulcerative gastritis and includes antibiotics and acid-reducing medications. Since most sick pets aren't eating, hospitalization with force-feeding and fluid therapy may be needed. Most ferrets will survive and completely recover with proper treatment.

Another wasting disease is called *proliferative colitis*. This disease is caused by a Campylobacter organism and is treated with antibiotics. Signs are similar to those seen with Helicobacter infection, and some ferrets may have both diseases. Therefore, it is best to treat all ferrets that are wasting away as if they have both diseases. Treatment is usually successful.

Gastrointestinal Foreign Bodies

Being curious creatures, ferrets are commonly affected by foreign objects causing gastrointestinal obstructions. Any objects can be investigated, chewed, and swallowed, but most commonly ferrets ingest rubber parts of shoes, furniture and mattress stuffing, rubber bands, erasers, and parts of dog and cat toys. These obstructions are difficult to diagnose unless the owner observes the ferret swallowing the object or sees a piece of the object missing. They are hard to identify on routine radiographs (X-rays). Common signs are the same as with many ferret diseases, and include lack of appetite, lethargy, diarrhea, and gradual body wasting. Vomiting is not always seen (unlike dogs and cats with gastrointestinal obstructions) but can be severe when present. Vomiting of a severe, projectile nature is suggestive of a complete obstruction.

Left untreated, the ferret will die from a perforation of its intestines and secondary peritonitis. Diagnosis is often made during exploratory surgery. If this malady is identified early, ferrets can recover without significant problems.

Another common cause of gastrointestinal obstruction is hairballs. These occur more commonly in older (one year and older) ferrets, whereas ingestion of foreign objects is more likely in young ferrets. Signs are similar to obstruction with other objects. All ferrets should regularly receive some type of hairball laxative product recommended by a veterinarian to decrease the chance of hairball obstructions.

Anal Sac Impactions

Like dogs and cats, a ferret has two sacs near its anus. These sacs contain glands that produce a foul-smelling secretion when the ferret has a bowel movement. These secretions impart an odor to the stool that is probably used in territorial marking and identification of the ferret.

Occasionally the sacs don't empty properly and will fill up. Most ferrets don't seem to show the same signs that dogs and cats with anal sac impactions exhibit, such as licking the rear end or scooting the rear end on the floor. Sometimes the stool will be thin and ribbon-like, and a portion of the rectum might prolapse (protrude) from the anus. Often no signs are seen until the sacs have abscessed and opened, which allows them to drain.

Treatment involves flushing the abscesses (lancing them open if necessary) and antibiotics. This disease is rarely seen, as most ferrets have these sacs removed early in life at the same time they are spayed or neutered in order to decrease their odor.

Enlarged Spleen

During a physical examination, the veterinarian may find an enlarged spleen. While not a sign of any one disease, it does indicate the need for further investigation. Several diseases that can result in splenic enlargement include inflammation of the spleen, malignant tumors, cancer, cardiomyopathy, and Aleutian disease. Obviously an enlarged spleen is a serious sign that indicates the need for complete laboratory testing to determine the cause.

Chapter 6

Rabbits

General Information

Rabbits make a nice alternative to a dog or cat. They are usually not aggressive (unlike some ferrets), don't have to be walked, and usually learn to use a litterbox quite easily. Their average lifespan is 5-10 years, and they reach breeding age at 6 months of age. Early spaying and neutering at 4-6 months of age is recommended to decrease both medical and behavioral problems. Rabbits are known for their easy breeding abilities; pregnancy lasts about 30 days and the average size litter is 4-10 bunnies.

Proper handling of rabbits is important. Rabbits have a lightweight skeleton compared to most animals. Their powerful back legs allow them to kick with a large amount of force, which can easily cause a rabbit to break its back if held improperly. This can result in euthanasia for the paralyzed rabbit. When carrying your pet, always support its hindquarters. If the rabbit struggles, it should be placed down immediately, given time to quiet itself, and picked up a few minutes later. *Never* pick up your rabbit by its ears. Have your veterinarian show you the proper way to restrain and carry your rabbit.

Some rabbits may become aggressive. Most often owners complain about their rabbit being agressive either toward them or toward another rabbit. The aggressiveness is usually noticed as the rabbit reaches puberty, commonly by six months of age. While this is usually associated with male rabbits (especially if two males are housed together), any rabbit can become aggressive toward the owner. Neutering or spaying may correct the problem.

Anatomical Interests

1. Rabbits have large ears, which give them an excellent sense of hearing. The ears also serve as a way for the rabbit to regulate its body temperature. The ears contain large veins which are often used for drawing blood for diagnostic testing.
2. Rabbits have a digestive tract that is adapted for digesting the large amount of fiber that is required in their diets.

3. Compared to other pets, a rabbit's skeleton is very light in relation to the rest of its body. This means that their bones fracture (break) more easily; carrying a rabbit improperly can predispose it to bone fractures.
4. Rabbits have two pairs of upper incisor teeth (the second pair is hidden behind the first).
5. Rabbits' teeth, like rodents', grow throughout the pet's life and may need periodic trimming by your veterinarian. Providing your rabbit with blocks of wood to chew on often prevents overgrown incisors, a common condition in pet rabbits.

Selecting your Pet

Rabbits can be purchased at pet stores or through breeders. Ideally, select a young bunny. The eyes and nose should be clear and free of any discharge that might indicate a respiratory infection. The rabbit should be curious and inquisitive. It should not be thin and emaciated. Check for the presence of wetness around the anus, which might indicate diarrhea. Also check for the presence of parasites such as fleas and ear mites (ear mites cause the production of waxy black matter in the ears). If possible, examine the rabbit's mouth for broken or overgrown incisors (front teeth), discolored gums (they should be light pink), and any obvious sores. Inquire as to whether the rabbit has been spayed or neutered; most have not been at the time of purchase. These operations should be performed by 4-6 months of age. Finally, inquire as to any guarantee of health offered by the seller.

The First Veterinary Visit

Your rabbit should be examined by a qualified veterinarian within 48 hours of purchase (this examination is often required by the seller or any guarantee is voided). Make sure the veterinarian has experience in treating rabbits. He should discuss housing, proper diet, and appropriate toys for the rabbit. A fecal sample should be examined for parasites. Go with a list of questions, and you'll start off on the right track. Rabbits require annual examinations and stool tests, although no annual vaccinations are required.

Housing

Rabbits should never be allowed to run loose in the house. They love to chew and can be very destructive to your house and furniture. There is always a chance of injury, such as chewing on an electrical cord. Your rabbit can be let out of its cage when you're in the room and can supervise and play with it. Like cats, they quickly learn to use a litterbox. Most owners use a portable dog or cat carrier as a cage and use a towel as bedding. Wire rabbit cages are also fine, but to decrease foot trauma (which results in a condition called "sore hocks"), it is recommended to cover at least half of the wire floor with toweling, plexiglass, or wood. Place the litterbox and ceramic or steel food and water bowls in the carrier (bowls are preferable to droppers for water, which must be inspected daily for clogging of the nipple). A concealed "hiding" area in the cage allows the rabbit to feel secure.

Diet

High-quality rabbit chows, pellets, and good quality hay (such as alfalfa, grass, or clover) make up the rabbit's diet. For rabbits less than one year old, pellets and hay should be available free choice, which means the rabbit is free to eat as much of each as it wishes. For animals over one year of age, hay, which provides fiber, should be available free choice and make up most of the diet. Pellets or chows can be offered at approximately 1/4 cup per 5 pounds of body weight. Overfeeding pellets to adult rabbits is a common cause of disease. Fresh water should be available at all times. Other items such as fruits and vegetables can be offered daily as well. Fruits and vegetables should be thought of as a supplement (think of fruits as a treat) and not as the sole diet. Therefore, limit their amount to no more than 20% of the diet, with vegetables making up most of this percentage. Fresh produce is best; make sure it's thoroughly washed prior to feeding. As with many pets, variety is the key, so offer small amounts of several items (avoid just cabbage, apples, and carrots). Avoid lettuce and celery as they are of little nutritional value. Anything dark green and leafy is loaded with vitamins and is a good supplement. Vitamin supplementation is not needed in most rabbits. Chew toys should be available; anything suited for dogs, such as Nylabones or well-boiled meat bones, are fine. Many owners offer their rabbits wood sticks to chew on, which helps control overgrown incisors.

Rabbits engage in coprophagy, which means they eat their own stool. This eating occurs at night, and these fecal pellets are different from the ones normally excreted and seen by the owners. These pellets serve as a source of nutrients, specifically vitamins, for the rabbit. Most owners never observe this behavior; if you do, remember that it is normal and necessary for the health of your rabbit.

Diseases

Pasteurella ("Snuffles")

Infection with Pasteurella bacteria is the most commonly seen disease in bunnies. Usually called "snuffles," the most common clinical signs are related to the eyes (discharge, redness, squinting) or nose (sneezing, discharge). Often the eyes and nose are affected at the same time. Pasteurella can infect other areas of the body as well. Ear infections (resulting in a head tilt), abscesses (seen as lumps on the body), and uterine infections (often only diagnosed during exploratory surgery) are also seen. Sudden death from septicemia (infection in the blood) is rare but can occur.

Most cases of snuffles are mild. Treatment involves antibiotics. Due to potential problems with many oral antibiotics, injections are often preferred. Eye drops and nose drops, prescribed by your doctor, may be needed in some cases.

Pasteurella is easy to treat but hard, if not impossible, to cure. As with kennel cough bacterium in dogs, many doctors feel that all rabbits have Pasteurella, but only some show signs. Many rabbits are chronically infected, just like some children always seem to have a cold. The disease is easily transmitted by close contact between rabbits; new rabbits should be isolated (for about one month) before introducing them to existing pets. Stressful situations, such as the introduction of a new pet, new diet, or overcrowding, can cause relapses. Litter should be changed regularly to prevent ammonia accumulation from the urine which can irritate the eyes and nasal tissue.

Diarrhea/Mucoid Enteropathy

Diarrhea is often seen in rabbits. While it can be due to coccidia (a one-cell protozoan) or incorrect usage of oral antibiotics, often the cause can't be determined. Rabbits eating a diet that is too high in carbohydrates (pellets) are more prone to develop intestinal problems than rabbits eating a high fiber (hay) diet.

Mucoid enteropathy is by definition a diarrheal disease of young rabbits that can easily be fatal. The diarrhea has a mucoid or gelatinous consistency.

Treatment for diarrheal conditions of rabbits is controversial and varies among veterinarians. As a rule, fiber in the diet is increased (often nothing but hay is offered for several weeks). Fluid and vitamin therapy are administered as needed.

Cystic Calculi (Bladder Stones)

Rabbits, like many pets, can develop bladder stones. Signs include urinating frequently, straining to urinate, and blood in the urine. Often the stones can be palpated (felt) by the veterinarian during the examination. Radiographs (X-rays) can confirm the diagnosis. Surgical removal of the stones cures the problem. Rabbits that have been eating too many pellets (this may contribute to stone formation) can be weaned onto a diet lower in pellets and higher in hay which may prevent stone recurrence.

Uterine Adenocarcinoma/Pyometra

Like dogs and cats, female rabbits should be spayed early in life (by 4-6 months of age). Whereas unspayed female dogs and cats often develop malignant breast cancer, and unspayed female ferrets die of fatal anemia, unspayed female rabbits often develop uterine cancer. The type of cancer is called uterine adenocarcinoma. This is a relatively common condition of older female rabbits. It's one of the diseases I most commonly suspect whenever I see any sick, unspayed female rabbit. Diagnosis is difficult and often only made during exploratory surgery.

If the rabbit doesn't have uterine adenocarcinoma (cancer), she often has pyometra. Pyometra, also common in unspayed dogs and cats, literally means "pus in the uterus." This infection can reveal itself through a vaginal discharge, but like adenocarcinoma is often diagnosed during exploratory surgery. To help prevent these conditions, early spaying of all female rabbits by 4-6 months of age is recommended. If you plan to breed your bunny, have it spayed after completion of all planned breeding.

Trichobezoars

Hairballs are relatively common in rabbits. Like cats and ferrets, rabbits are very clean animals and love to groom themselves. Occasionally, a lot of hair is swallowed during the grooming procedure and forms a ball in the stomach. Rabbits can't vomit, and if the hair doesn't pass through their intestinal tract they will develop an obstruction.

Hairballs are so common that this is the number one condition I suspect anytime I examine a rabbit that is lethargic and not eating. Diagnosis can be made by taking radiographs (X-rays) of the stomach. If the owner is sure the rabbit has not eaten within 24 hours and the radiographs reveal food in the stomach, we can be pretty sure something is causing an obstruction, and it's often a hairball. Sometimes, the diagnosis is only made during exploratory surgery.

For very early, mild cases, injections of drugs that alter intestinal motility may allow the obstruction to pass. Otherwise, surgery is needed to remove the hairball. The earlier surgery is performed, the better; mortality (death) from surgery is often 50% or higher!

Many doctors feel that giving rabbits cat hairball medicine on a regular basis helps prevent the problem. Feeding rabbits a diet high in hay (fiber) also helps prevent hairballs and other intestinal problems. Daily brushing is also essential for removing excess dead hair.

Nails

Rabbits have sharp nails, and owners are easily scratched when handling their pets. Rabbits' back feet are usually the culprits as they are the most powerful. Owners are most often scratched when placing a rabbit back into its cage or down onto the floor. Supporting the rabbit's hindquarters during the entire lifting, carrying, and replacing regimen will usually eliminate the problem.

Periodic nail trimming (have your doctor show you the proper technique) is important. *Rabbits should not be declawed except in extreme cases!*

Skin Diseases

Rabbits get several skin diseases, including bacterial infections, ringworm, and flea infestations. Ringworm usually appears as circular patterns of hair loss with scaling at the periphery of the circle. Your veterinarian will do a skin scraping to make sure mange isn't the culprit; a fungal culture will confirm the diagnosis of ringworm. Treatment for ringworm involves topical medications, oral medications, or medicated shampoo as determined by the severity of the signs.

Bacterial infections are diagnosed by skin biopsy and culture; appropriate antibiotics (usually injections) and medicated shampoo are usually used to treat the conditions.

Rabbits can get fleas just like dogs and cats. Your veterinarian will recommend safe products for use on your pet as well as in the environment.

Parasites

The most commonly seen parasites of rabbits include mange, ear mites, fleas, and coccidia.

Mange, or Cheyletiella dermatitis ("walking dandruff"), is seen as hair loss and the accumulation of scales on the body that resemble dandruff. Upon close observation, the "dandruff" moves; the dandruff is actually the mites (parasites) moving among the fur. Diagnosis is confirmed by skin scrapings, and treatment involves medicated shampooing. While it usually doesn't affect people, it can be transmitted to other rabbits.

Ear mites are a common parasite of rabbits. Usually a dark, crusty material is seen in the ears, and often rabbits shake their heads and scratch their ears. Diagnosis is made by microscopic examination of an ear swab; treatment utilizes either an injectable drug or topical medication. Often a flea spray is used to kill those mites that temporarily live outside the ears. Ear mites are very transmissible to other animals; people are rarely affected.

Coccidia are parasites that infect the intestines or liver and are diagnosed with a microscopic examination of the feces. Diarrhea can be seen, although many cases are diagnosed in a normal rabbit during the annual physical examination and fecal testing. The liver form of the disease often causes lack of appetite, lethargy, or even sudden death. Treatment is with oral medication.

Overgrown Incisors

Like rodents', rabbits' front teeth (the incisors) grow continuously throughout life. Usually, chewing on food, wood blocks, and toys keeps them a normal length. Occasionally, this is not sufficient and the incisors will overgrow. Rabbits with overgrown incisors may stop eating or drool excessively. Looking into the mouth allows you to easily detect the problem. Your doctor can treat the problem by filing the incisors under anesthesia. Clipping the teeth with nail trimmers or wire cutters, once a popular treatment, is no longer recommended because the incisors can fracture easily, resulting in pain and infection.

Pododermatitis ("Sore Hocks")

The hocks are essentially a rabbit's ankles. When a rabbit is sitting, which it does most of the time, its hocks are in contact with the floor of its cage. Often, wire-floored cages put too much pressure on the hocks, causing them to lose hair, turn red, and become ulcerated and painful. The condition is usually prevented by supplying rabbits that live in wire cages with another surface to sit on, such as a piece of wood, plexiglass, or a towel covering at least half of the wire cage. Treatment requires antibacterial medications to clean the infected hocks. Providing soft bedding is essential to allow the sores to heal. If the condition is diagnosed early, the hocks usually can be treated without much effort, however, this can easily become a chronic, difficult-to-treat condition.

Antibiotic Toxicity

Several references in publications discuss antibiotic toxicities in rabbits. Some of the reports warn against using *any* oral antibiotics in rabbits, whereas others mention specific problems with oral drugs such as penicillins or lincomycin. I have not had any problems with oral antibiotics I have used to treat sick rabbits. As a rule, to be safe, I usually recommend that owners use injectable medications when possible; most owners can easily be taught to give their rabbits injections.

Chapter 7

Pocket Pets

(Small Rodents)

General Information

Pocket pets (hamsters, rats, mice, gerbils, and guinea pigs) are very popular pets. They make good first pets for young children and as a rule are easy to care for. Compared to dogs and cats, they have a shorter lifespan (two to five years depending upon the species); young children should be told this so that the "sudden death" of a three-year-old pet isn't unexpected. As with any pet, they do occasionally get sick, and their illnesses are often severe. Regular veterinary examinations and fecal tests can prevent some problems; at the very least, any new pet should be examined within 48 hours of purchase. This "new pet" exam is critical to detect signs of disease and help new pet owners get off on the right foot. So many problems are caused by misinformation; the first veterinary visit can help prevent well-intentioned owners from doing the wrong thing and ultimately contributing to the pet's early death.

For the sake of convenience, since much of the information concerning one species of pocket pet is applicable to all pocket pets, this general information will be discussed first.

Species differences, especially in the area of diseases, will be discussed under the appropriate section.

VITAL STATISTICS

	Life Expectancy (Years)	Avg. Weight (Grams)	Breeding Age (Days)	Gestation* (Days)
Guinea Pig	4-8	750	90-150	59-72
Rat	1-3	350	90-110	20-22
Mouse	1-3	40	42-49	17-21
Hamster	1-3	125	48-56	15-18
Gerbil	2-4	90	70-90	24-26

* Gestation is the period of time the pet is pregnant.

Hamster

Guinea Pig

Mice

Gerbil

Rat

Anatomical Interests

Common to all of the pocket pets is the fact that the front teeth, the incisors, grow continuously throughout the pet's life. Overgrown incisors are a frequent problem and can be prevented by allowing the pet access to pieces of wood and other chew objects. Treatment involves filing by the veterinarian, often under anesthesia.

Rodents are herbivorous animals, and the digestive tract is similar to that of other plant-eaters such as horses and cattle.

Guinea Pigs

1. No obvious tail is present.
2. Unlike other rodents, only one pair of mammary glands is present.
3. The guinea pig is the only pocket pet with premolar teeth. Unlike most mammals, the young are precocious at birth, meaning they are fully developed, born with hair, and the eyes open.
4. Guinea pigs rarely bite, which makes them ideal pets. However, they do squeal when handled.

Mice

1. Porphyrin from the harderian glands around the eyes causes tears and nasal secretions to appear red.
2. The spleen of males is larger than the spleen of females.
3. The mammary glands extend along the sides and back of the pet, and therefore breast cancer can appear as a lump *anywhere* on the body.
4. Young mice are born hairless with their eyes closed.

Rats

1. Rats do not have tonsils or a gall bladder.
2. Similar to mice, rats have a harderian gland that produces red tears and nasal secretions.
3. The young are born hairless with their eyes closed.

Hamsters

1. Hip glands, which appear as a black dot on each hip, are present in males. They are used for territorial marking and are poorly developed in females.
2. Hamsters have a cheek pouch on each side of the inside of the mouth. Food, and often baby hamsters, are temporarily stored here!
3. Hamsters are the most aggressive (meanest) of all the pocket pets and often bite.
4. Hamsters can hibernate. A sleeping hamster should be awakened carefully!

Gerbils

1. Since gerbils are desert animals, they have a very low water requirement.
2. Due to the low water intake, gerbils urinate very small amounts.
3. Gerbils usually mate for life; they should be paired before sexual maturity.
4. Many gerbils exhibit mild spontaneous seizures (epilepsy), especially when startled. These usually don't require treatment.
5. Gerbils have high blood cholesterol and lipid (fat) levels but do not show arteriosclerosis.

Selecting Your Pet

Most owners will buy their pocket pets locally through a pet store. Avoid sick-looking animals. Don't try to a "Good Samaritan." Remember that with exotic pets, if it looks sick, it's really dying! Trying to nurse a sick pocket pet back to health after purchasing it will rarely work. Just the stress of the new environment and feeding is often enough to kill it. So, start out right with a healthy pet. Always inquire about the guarantee in case the pet is found to be unhealthy.

The pocket pet should have no discharge from the eyes, nose, or mouth. If you can open the mouth (without being bitten!), make sure the front teeth, the incisors, have not overgrown (they should form a nice, even fit). The animal should seem frisky and try to run and resist handling to some extent. No coughing, sneezing, or wheezing should be present. Examine the rectal area. It should be dry and free of diarrhea or caked-on stool. Ask the employee for help in determining the animal's sex. Keep in mind that pet store employees may know little more than you about the pet: the sex can be correctly determined during your pet's first veterinary visit.

The First Veterinary Visit

Within 48 hours of purchase, your pet should be examined by a veterinarian knowledgeable in the treatment of pocket pets. The visit includes determining the animal's weight, as well as checking lumps or bumps. The animal is examined for signs of dehydration and starvation. A fecal test is done to check for internal parasites. The veterinarian can also determine the sex of your pet.

No vaccines are required for pocket pets. Most of the visit will probably be a question-and-answer session. We spend an average of 30 minutes with all new owners of exotic pets and give them a handout as well as suggest several good books to read. If all turns out well, your pet will be given a clean bill of health. Like all pets, pocket pets should be examined annually and have their stool tested for parasites annually.

Housing

It is most convenient to house pocket pets in a glass aquarium, although cages are available specifically for these pets. Wooden cages are not suitable as these rodents love to chew and can really destroy their homes. The cages can be left open at the top providing that the pet can't escape and other pets (such as the family dog or cat) can't get to the pocket pet. *All pocket pets, being rodents, are masters of escape;* therefore, their cages must be escape-proof. Letting a pocket pet have free run of the house is discouraged due to potential for injury and death to the pet, as well as the possibility of furniture damage. Your pet can be handled outside of the cage if care is used (supervise young children). The environmental temperature should be kept between 65 and 85 degrees. Since rodents like to burrow, it is recommended that some type of hiding place be provided for them in the cage. Round, hollow objects can be purchased at the pet stores, or cleaned cans (such as an orange juice can) or paper towel cardboard rolls can be provided. If using a can, be sure there are no exposed metal pieces that can cause injury; with paper towel or toilet paper rolls, expect the pet will probably chew these up rather quickly, so they will need to be replaced fairly often.

Wood shavings, such as pine or cedar, are usually provided for bedding material. Shredded paper or towels are also fine. Avoid sawdust, sand, or dirt. The cage should be cleaned and the bedding changed as often as it gets dirty, but at least weekly. A major cause of respiratory disease in a pocket pets is poor environmental ventilation, which allows ammonia from the urine to build up and irritate the pet's airways. A frequently cleaned, well-ventilated environment is important in controlling respiratory infections. Any toys should be cleaned weekly as well.

Cage toys can provide psychological stimulation as well as exercise for the pocket pets. Tubes and mazes are popular, as are exercise wheels. I am concerned about "open track" exercise wheels, because I have seen several rodents, mostly hamsters, become injured by getting a foot trapped in the wheel. Those hamsters with severe injuries, which are the majority, are either euthanized or require a leg amputation. While not every animal with an exercise wheel will be injured, it is a risk I advise you not to take. The safest wheel is composed of plastic and has no openings in the track ("solid track") where a foot can get caught.

Group Housing

While it is most common to have a single or occasionally a pair of animals, clients often inquire about housing several pets together. Several generalities can be made regarding group housing:

1. If a male and female are housed together, especially if they were paired at an early age, mating will occur.
2. Never house different species in the same cage (i.e., a rat and a mouse).
3. Some species should not be housed in the same area (such as rabbits and guinea pigs), as one species may carry an infectious organism that could be fatal to another species.
4. If a pocket pet has been housed alone, it is best not to introduce a new friend to it, as fighting is likely to occur. The exception would be introducing breeding animals (breeding is not covered in this book).

Guinea Pigs

Guinea pigs can be housed together.

Hamsters

Hamsters are best housed individually. Sexually mature females are aggressive to each other and to males.

Mice

Male mice are usually housed alone. Female mice rarely fight and are often housed together. Newly assembled male groups, new males entering established territories, and mice previously housed alone are more likely to fight.

Rats

Unlike mice, rats rarely fight and can be housed in groups. Occasionally, females that have just given birth may fight with other females.

Gerbils

Gerbils are usually housed individually. A monogamous pair can be formed if the male and female are bonded before 8 weeks of age. The pair should not, as a rule, be separated.

Feeding

Pocket pets can be fed a good, high-quality rodent chow (pelleted food) available at pet stores. The diets containing seeds and nuts are *not* recommended. If offered these good-tasting seeds and nuts which are high in fat, many rodents will eat these instead of the formulated pellets. Seeds and nuts can be offered as an occasional treat (less than 10% of the daily diet). Fresh, well-cleaned vegetables and occasionally a small amount of fruit can be offered as well. Leafy green vegetables (not lettuce or celery) can be offered, as well as yellow and orange vegetables. Bread and meat (tuna, chicken, etc.) can also be offered. The total daily amount of these "people foods" should not run more than 10% of the diet. Thus, the pets should eat mainly pellets (90% of the diet), vegetables and fruits (5-10%), and occasionally a few seeds or nuts as treats. Many owners offer the food in heavy, spill-proof ceramic crocks, although feeders can be purchased and attached to the cage. I also suggest offering hay (such as alfalfa cubes or clover) free choice to the pets as a source of fiber.

Water should be available 24 hours a day and is usually provided in sipper tubes available at pet stores, although it can be placed in spill-proof crocks. The water should be replaced daily and the tubes (specifically the end the pet drinks from) inspected daily for blockage that can develop if the pets spits food into the sipper tube.

Diseases

One of the most common complaints I deal with, regardless of whether the pet is a guinea pig, hamster, or other pocket pet, is what we veterinarians call "ADR." ADR is a slang term for "ain't doing right." The owner complains that the pet is anorectic (isn't eating), lethargic (isn't moving), and just overall is acting sick.

Unfortunately, while this type of complaint does confirm that *something* is wrong, it doesn't give me any clues as to *what* is wrong. Any disease can cause an animal to not feel good. As with other exotic pets, the sooner a pocket pet is seen and treated, the better the prognosis (chance of cure). Pet store antibiotics are ineffective against diseases of pocket pets and should *never* be used.

So if we know that the pet is sick but we don't know why it's sick, just what do we do? What answers can I offer a worried owner of a sick pocket pet?

Well, to start with, there are some diagnostic tests we can do on these pets. We are limited, however, by two things: the size of the animal and the amount of money a client will spend. It's almost impossible to draw any amount of blood on a hamster or mouse, but we can do a urinalysis, fecal analysis, and radiographs (X-rays). We can do some diagnostic testing, but often owners will not pay $100 for testing on a pet that they can replace for $5-$10. Therefore, we often have to "shoot from the hip" and make an educated guess as to the cause of the disease and possible treatment.

Knowing that certain species are more prone to one disease than another species, veterinarians can make a rational decision regarding treatment and prognosis. As is true with any pet, the more we can do diagnostically, the greater our chance of success. Since many owners don't bring in their pocket pets until the pet has been sick for several days, and since so many of these pets have been "home-treated" with pet store antibiotics, the prognosis is always guarded.

Pocket pets, like other exotics, don't show signs of disease until late in the course of the illness. This is called the "preservation response." In the wild, an animal can't afford to act sick every time it's a little under the weather. If it did, the other members of its pack would kill it or force it out of the group, where it would be easy prey for predators. So, when a pocket pet is sick, it doesn't act sick until it can't hide its illness any more. What this means is that by the time your pet is acting sick, it has really been sick for some time. That's why your pet needs to see a veterinarian at the first sign of illness!

Most of the illnesses in pocket pets are ultimately treated with either oral or injectable (often preferred) medications. Since some pocket pets, such as guinea pigs, are extremely susceptible to fatal side effects from any antibiotics, we are often limited in the number of choices we have for antibacterial therapy. Nevertheless, with early intervention we can offer hope for many of the diseases seen in pocket pets.

As I've said, many pets are brought in for the "ADR" complaint. There are specific diseases that occur more frequently in one species or another, and for the sake of convenience I'll cover these in a moment. Some complaints are applicable to all pocket pets. So a brief discussion of these is in order first.

Anorexia

Loss of appetite is commonly seen with most diseases. The first thing I think about with any pet that isn't eating is whether or not it *can* eat. Is there any oral cavity disease? Since pocket pets are rodents, and since all rodents have teeth that grow continuously throughout their lives, I like to check the teeth. Sometimes owners complain of the pet drooling or having a wet chin ("slobbers"). Often the front teeth, the incisors, have overgrown and are interfering with eating. Sometimes the back teeth, the molars, have overgrown and make eating painful. Trimming the incisors is done under anesthesia with a Dremel tool. Formerly we used nail clippers or wire cutters without anesthesia, but this often led to broken teeth, which resulted in more problems. The diagnosis of overgrown molars usually requires anesthesia and radiographs (X-rays); treatment is trimming of the molars (which is often difficult) under anesthesia. This malady can often be prevented by offering something for the pet to chew, such as a block of wood.

Gastrointestinal Obstructions

Pets eating hay (fiber) in their diet rarely have gastrointestinal problems such as obstructions or diarrhea. Obstructions, including hairballs, can lodge anywhere in the intestinal tract or stomach. Diagnosis is made with radiographs and often surgery is needed for treatment.

Respiratory Infections

Different microorganisms will be discussed for each species, but respiratory infections, including pneumonia, are common in pocket pets. Signs include nasal and/or ocular (eye) discharge, wheezing, coughing, and open-mouth breathing. Radiographs can be used to confirm a diagnosis, and antibiotic treatment is indicated. Supportive care, including force-feeding and subcutaneous fluids (fluids given under the skin), may be needed.

Diarrhea

Commonly seen in pocket pets, the actual cause of diarrhea may be difficult to determine. A fecal analysis can be performed to check for parasites (worms). Supportive care is needed, as is increasing the amount of fiber (hay) in the diet. Every attempt should be made to prevent diarrhea, as it is often difficult to treat and can be fatal. Feeding a source of fiber at an early age is important, as is avoiding giving the wrong antibiotics to certain rodents. Administering the wrong antibiotic can cause a fatal diarrhea due to disruption of normal gastrointestinal flora.

Tyzzer's Disease

This is an infectious gastrointestinal disease which can be seen in any of the pocket pets. It is a bacterial disease usually seen in young pets, although stressed animals of any age can get the infection. Diarrhea, dehydration, and death are commonly seen. Treatment is usually unrewarding, but antibiotics might help prevent an outbreak.

External Parasites

Caused by a microscopic mite, different types of mange occur in different animals. Clinically, hair loss, occasionally with crusting and itching, are seen. Lice also cause similar signs. As a rule, parasites that infect pocket pets do not infect people. They can infect other pocket pets, so isolation of the affected animal is important. Diagnosis is made through lab tests such as skin scrapings or skin biopsies. Treatment often involves medicated shampoos or dips as prescribed by your veterinarian.

Dermatomycosis (Ringworm)

Most mammals can contact ringworm, which is a fungal infection of the skin and hair. The type of fungus that affects rodents is usually different from the one which normally affects other pets and people, although all can be susceptible to rodent ringworm (wash your hands thoroughly after handling infected rodents). Signs include hair loss (usually from the head and face) and crusty lesions. Treatment involves medicated baths and oral antifungal drugs.

Barbering

Many rodents chew on the hair of their cagemates. Separating the animals prevents the problem.

Foot Necrosis/Gangrene

While not seen as commonly as in smaller birds, this condition does occur in rodents. It is caused by the fine fiber or thread nesting material (or bedding) commonly available in pet stores. The pets play with this stuff, the fine thread gets wrapped around a toe or foot or leg, and within hours the body part is swelling and turning red. This is similar to what happens when you wind a thread tightly around your own finger. If not caught immediately, the swelling progresses to death (necrosis) of the limb followed shortly by gangrene. Affected limbs are swollen and various shades of shades of red, purple, blue and black. In some animals, amputations might be curative. Often, the high cost of the surgery ($100-$200) forces owners to choose euthanasia for these pets. To prevent this condition, do not use this fine bedding or nesting material. Shredded tissue works perfectly.

Guinea Pigs

Vitamin C Deficiency (Scurvy)

Unlike many pets, guinea pigs can't make their own vitamin C. This means it must be provided to the pet. Even though guinea pig pellets are fortified with vitamin C, owners should still supplement with vitamin C in the water. This is because vitamin C is an unstable vitamin and quickly disappears from the pellets. Crush 200 mg of vitamin C tablets (available at pharmacies or health food stores) and mix with 1 liter of water. This needs to be made fresh daily and offered in the sipper tube as the source of water. Fresh green vegetables also provide supplemented vitamin C. Signs of vitamin C deficiency (scurvy) include loss of appetite, swollen, painful joints, reluctance to move, lack of resistance to infection, and occasional bleeding from the gums. Any sick guinea pig should be given a vitamin C injection as part of its treatment.

Dystocia

Dystocia means "difficult birth," and sometimes develops in pregnant guinea pigs. The pubic symphysis, the area of the pelvis that connects the left and right halves of the hips, widen in female guinea pigs to allow them to give birth. This only happens if the female is bred before 9 months of age; otherwise, the symphysis calcifies and the spreading that is needed to allow a normal birth can't happen. For this reason female guinea pigs intended for breeding should be bred before 9 months of age, ideally at 6 months of age. Guinea pigs having dystocia often require a Caesarean section.

Pregnancy Toxemia

Pregnant guinea pigs can experience a toxemia not unlike that experienced by pregnant women (similar to eclampsia). It usually occurs in the latter stages of pregnancy and often in obese guinea pigs. The condition can be associated with any type of stress, such as a change in diet, environment, or housing. Affected females become ill quickly and exhibit loss of appetite, lethargy, difficulty breathing, weight loss, and depression. Death can occur within 24 hours. Treatment involves supportive care and glucose solutions. Prevention is accomplished by avoiding stress in pregnant females and avoiding high-fat diets, such as seeds and nuts.

Cervical Lymphadenitis ("Lumps")

"Lumps" is an infection, usually with a Streptococcus bacterium, of the lymph nodes located underneath the jaw (mandible). The predominant sign is a lump under the jaw; if not detected early, the pig can lose its appetite and become lethargic. Treatment includes opening and flushing the abscess and antibiotic therapy.

Respiratory Infections (Pneumonia)

All rodents are susceptible to various bacteria and other organisms that cause respiratory infections. Left untreated, these infections can easily progress to pneumonia, a life-threatening lung infection. Signs of respiratory infections include nasal or eye discharge, noisy breathing, and open-mouth breathing. The sicker animals often stop eating and become lethargic. Bordetella is one such bacterium that affects guinea pigs; it can be fatal. Since rabbits carry this organism without showing signs of illness, it is recommended that rabbits and guinea pigs not be housed together.

Hyperthermia

Guinea pigs are very susceptible to heat stroke from high ambient temperatures. As a rule, the temperature should be no higher than 80 degrees, and the cage should be well-ventilated and the humidity kept below 70 degrees. Signs of heat stroke include panting, slobbering, weakness, convulsions, and refusal to move. Treatment involves immediately cooling the pet with cool water baths or sprays. Ideally, the temperature should be monitored with an in-cage thermometer.

Antibiotic Toxicities

Like many rodents, guinea pigs are sensitive to certain antibiotics. Several antibiotics can be fatal to guinea pigs; this is true whether the antibiotics are given orally, by injection, or topically (on the skin). Toxic antibiotics include penicillin and related drugs, bacitracin, erythromycin, lincomycin, tylosin, and streptomycin. Owners should *never* administer antibiotics to their guinea pigs without first consulting a veterinarian with experience in pocket pet medicine.

Coccidiosis

Coccidia are one-cell protozoan parasites that live in the intestinal tract. Signs of infection include diarrhea, weakness, and weight loss. A fecal examination (which should be performed annually) can detect the parasite, which is treated with oral medication.

Mice and Rats

Respiratory Disease (Mycoplasmosis)

Probably the most common malady in many pocket pets is respiratory disease. In mice and rats, this is often caused by a mycoplasma, a type of bacterium. Signs of infection include sneezing, nasal or ocular (eye) discharge, labored and audible breathing (usually only heard with a severe case resulting in pneumonia), and occasionally red tears. Treatment includes antibiotics, often for an extended length of time. Making sure the environment is clean and well-ventilated is important, as ammonia vapors from rodent urine often irritate the respiratory tract, allowing the disease to develop. Other agents, such as Pasteurella and Streptococcus bacteria, can also cause pneumonia. Many of the antibiotics that kill the Mycoplasma organism will also kill these other bacteria.

Sialodacryoadenitis ("Red Tears")

Red tears can be a result of a viral disease, mycoplasmosis, or as a sign of stress. Often it is hard to tell what is actually causing the problem. Many clients call with the complaint of "blood coming from the animal's eyes." In the viral infection, usually the salivary and tear glands are involved. Because rodents have porphyrins (pigments) in their tears, any discharge will be seen as red tears. Treatment is symptomatic and involves topical eye medication.

Mammary Neoplasia (Breast Cancer)

Rats and mice frequently develop tumors, and many of them are breast tumors. Amazingly, breast tissue in these pets covers most of the body, so breast cancer can even appear as a lump on the back of the pet! While usually benign, early removal is indicated, as these lumps can grow quite large and become uncomfortable for the pet and even ulcerate and become infected.

Mice Only

Antibiotic Toxicities

Procaine and streptomycin are fatal to mice, as is chloroform (an older type of anesthetic which is rarely used anymore).

Viral Diseases

While not commonly diagnosed in private practice, there are several viral diseases that mice can acquire. These include mouse pox (which causes dead areas of the tail and limbs), Sendai virus infection (often a fatal respiratory disease), hepatitis, leukemia, and a rotaviral infection of infant mice which causes gastrointestinal disease manifested by yellow, pasty feces.

Rats Only

Ringtail

Rats that are kept in environments with a low humidity (less than 20%) can develop circular constrictions of their tails. The tail often dies and falls off in the area of the constriction. The condition is often seen in the winter when heating systems are in use. The humidity for all rodents should be kept at least 50% throughout the year.

Hamsters

Pneumonia

This is often due to a Streptococcus or Pasteurella infection and is seen as a nasal and ocular (eye) discharge, wheezing, and open-mouth breathing. These animals require immediate attention and often die within a few days (even if treated).

Proliferative Ileitis ("Wet Tail")

The most serious intestinal disease of hamsters, wet tail is caused by a Campylobacter bacterium. Usually, 3- to 6-week-old hamsters are affected and show signs of lethargy, loss of appetite, unkempt hair coat, watery (sometimes bloody) diarrhea, and a wet anal and tail area. This disease requires immediate treatment including fluid therapy, antibiotics, and hospitalization. Animals may die even with early, aggressive treatment.

Infected Cheek Pouches

Hamsters have a cheek pouch on the inside of their mouths on the left and right cheek areas. These can become infected and even develop cancer. Abscesses can be treated with surgical drainage and antibiotics; cancerous lesions may be amenable to surgical removal depending upon their size. Any persistent swelling in the cheek area should be checked by your doctor.

Mange

Hamsters suffer from demodectic mange more than any of the pocket pets. This microscopic parasite lives in and infects hair follicles; infection causes hair loss, occasionally scaly skin, and sometimes itching. The parasite is diagnosed through skin scrapings or biopsies. Treatment utilizes a medicated shampoo. Mange in older hamsters often signals the presence of a severe internal disease, such as cancer or kidney disease.

Antibiotic Toxicities

Fatal reactions can occur in hamsters treated with penicillin, amoxicillin, ampicillin, erythromycin, streptomycin, and lincocin.

Fractures

Fractures of the legs (broken legs) are very common and usually result from injuries sustained on exercise wheels. Mild injuries may heal on their own; severe injuries require amputation of the leg or euthanasia. Only solid-bottom exercise wheels should be used in the cage.

Cancer

Cancer is common in older hamsters. Tumors of the thyroid and adrenal glands are common, as are tumors of the female reproductive tract. Hamsters also get cancer of the bone marrow called lymphosarcoma. Due to the difficulty in diagnosing and treating cancer in pocket pets, as well as the cost of these procedures, hamsters with cancer are often euthanized.

Gerbils

Compared with the other pocket pets, gerbils are rarely afflicted with diseases.

Staph Dermatitis

A staph bacterial skin infection can occur on the muzzle and nose of gerbils. It is seen as areas of hair loss and moisture. Treatment involves antibiotics.

Cancer

The most common types of cancers affecting gerbils are cancers of the ovaries and skin.

Seizures

The gerbil is unique among rodents in that spontaneous, epileptic-type seizures can occur, often after handling the pet. Most gerbils do not require medication for the seizures.

Muzzle Dermatitis

This is similar to, and often difficult to differentiate from, the staph dermatitis previously mentioned. In addition to a staph infection, muzzle alopecia (hair loss) can result from a parasitic infection called mange, or from trauma, such as that which occurs from the gerbil constantly rubbing its snout on the feeders or the cage itself.

Antibiotic Toxicities

Most antibiotics are safe in gerbils, but streptomycin is fatal.

Zoonotic Diseases

Zoonotic diseases are diseases that can be transmitted from animals to people. Thankfully, few such diseases are cause for concern in rodents.

The most commonly asked question I get is "Can I get rabies from my pocket pet?" While it is possible that any warm-blooded animal can contract, and therefore spread, rabies, it is highly unlikely that a pet rodent or even a wild one would transmit rabies to a person. Therefore we usually aren't concerned with contracting rabies from a rodent bite.

Any animal bite can, of course, cause an infection. All bites should be immediately and thoroughly cleaned with soap and water; a physician should be consulted regarding the need for a tetanus booster.

Salmonella, a bacterial infection causing intestinal problems, is a possible threat from any pet. People and pets can carry this organism in their feces without showing any clinical signs of the disease. Proper hygiene, such as thorough hand washing after handling pets and cleaning their cages, is important in disease prevention (make sure all children follow this procedure as well).

Hymenolepsis, the dwarf tapeworm, is a potential but unlikely cause of human disease. Since it is spread through feces, good hygiene is essential for prevention.

Tularemia, a disease associated with wild rabbits and squirrels, is extremely rare in domesticated pet rodents.

Plague, a dreaded disease, is not a problem with pet rodents but can be a big problem with wild ones, especially rats.

Lymphocytic choriomeningitis, a viral infection, has rarely been a problem in people. The virus, most commonly isolated from hamsters and guinea pigs, enters the body through an open wound or the respiratory passages. The disease is very rare but is fatal.

While this list of diseases seems menacing, zoonotic diseases from rodents are extremely rare. If you're considering a pocket pet, don't be frightened by these diseases. Use common sense and good hygiene, and the worst you'll probably get is a bite that can become infected if deep enough or if not properly cleaned.

Chapter 8

Birds

General Information

There are many species of birds popularly kept as pets. Since each one is a little different, a chapter could be devoted to each species in order for a bird owner to become thoroughly acquainted with his pet. However, that is beyond the scope of this introductory book. Instead, I have chosen to present information that is common to all species of pet birds, such as housing, feeding, and general care.

While birds do get "bird diseases" that are different from "dog diseases" and "cat diseases," each species of bird is commonly afflicted with some diseases that another species of bird rarely contracts. In discussing diseases, I will mention the most commonly seen conditions at our hospital, as well as the diseases most often affecting the less expensive, smaller species of birds commonly kept as pets (budgerigars, incorrectly referred to as "parakeets," and cockatiels).

Anatomical Interests

1. Birds do not have diaphragms. Breathing is accomplished by expanding the ribs. Therefore, when holding a bird, hold it snugly to prevent movement but take care not to restrict its breathing movements.

2. Birds have a cleft palate. The cleft, called the choana, is a common site to take gram stain and culture samples for disease diagnosis. In birds with diseases, especially those on a vitamin-deficient diet, the choana is often abnormal in appearance and covered with pus or abscesses.
3. Most birds are not sexually dimorphic, which means that the males and females look alike. Some exceptions do exist, such as with Eclectus parrots, where the males are green and the females are red.
4. Birds have feathers (which are modified scales, relating them to reptiles) as opposed to hair.
5. Some of the bones in a bird's body are pneumatic, meaning they contain air (through communication with the air sacs). This allows for a lighter skeleton, essential for flying.
6. Most of the gaseous exchange during respiration occurs in sacs called air sacs rather than in the lungs. These air sacs are located mainly in the bird's chest and abdominal cavities. Some of these air sacs enter bones, which makes the skeletal system light, allowing for easy flying.
7. Birds have a renal portal system. This allows blood from the legs to be filtered through the kidneys prior entering the general circulation. Clinically, this means infections of the legs can cause severe, generalized illness, and it also means injectable medications may be degraded if given in the leg muscles. Injections are therefore usually given in the large breast (pectoral) muscles.
8. Birds have two "stomachs": a true glandular stomach called the proventriculus, where digestion begins, and a muscular stomach called the ventriculus or gizzard, which grinds the food.

Cockatoo

Cockatiel

Peach-faced love bird

9. Birds do not have lips but instead have powerful beaks used in obtaining and "chewing" food; the beak and mobile tongue function as a third foot due to their dexterity.
10. Scales cover the feet of birds.
11. Most birds have a crop, a dilated pouch of the esophagus. The crop functions as a temporary storage area for food. From the crop the food can be transported to the stomach or regurgitated for feeding baby birds. Crop infections and impactions are commonly seen in birds.
12. Birds have a four-chambered heart.
13. Birds have no external "ears" but do have ear openings along the side of the head. These openings are normally covered with feathers.

Budgerigars ("budgies" are often incorrectly called "parakeets")

Selecting Your Pet

Hand-raised baby birds make the best pets. They cost considerably more but come already tame. Avoid inexpensive birds (I'm mainly referring to parrots that should cost $300 and up) that are often available on roadsides or at flea markets for $50-$100. These inexpensive birds are usually smuggled illegally into this country and are probably loaded with infectious diseases. Many of these birds die within hours of purchase, and often the seller is nowhere to be found after the sale. Good things aren't cheap, and cheap things aren't good!

The ideal bird for most first-time owners is a budgerigar ("budgie," erroneously called a "parakeet") or a cockatiel. These smaller birds make ideal pets for first-timers, and are easy to raise. Even if not purchased as hand-raised babies, these birds can usually be hand-tamed by first-time owners who exhibit patience and work with the birds on a daily basis. Other small birds (hand-raised) suitable for first-time owners include lovebirds, gray-cheeked parakeets, and some of the conures. Canaries and finches are fine too, but these birds usually are more for observing than playing with.

Most first-time owners should not purchase any of the bigger parrots or cockatoos. These birds are often too much bird for a first-time owner to deal with. Additionally, these birds require a large amount of interaction with their owners and often develop behavioral problems (especially feather picking) if not given the amount of attention they demand. Start out with a smaller bird and work up to a larger one!

Hand-raised babies are taken from the nest at a very early age and therefore imprint upon people. These birds often think they are people and don't require the company of another bird (some might not know what to do with another bird!). Since birds are flock creatures, you are becoming a part of their flock and must give them daily interaction and attention. Birds that are not hand-raised, except for the smaller birds such as budgies and cockatiels, are usually harder to tame and require the experience and patience of someone familiar with and comfortable with working with a large bird. Since this is labor-intensive, hand-raised birds cost more than wild-caught birds or those not hand-raised.

Birds can be purchased at pet shops or through breeders (often the local bird club can recommend a member who is currently raising a clutch of baby birds). As with any pet purchase, avoid birds that appear ill, fluffed up, sleepy (many baby birds sleep a lot and this is normal), or have abnormal droppings. Avoid purchasing from a breeder or store whose environment is unclean. Ideally, the bird should already be weaned (no longer being hand-fed); hand-feeding is time consuming and can be difficult for first-time owners.

Most birds are not sexually dimorphic, which means males and females look identical. With budgies, the males generally have a blue cere (the colored, fleshy part of the body just above the beak that contains the nasal openings) and the females have a pink or brown cere. This is not 100% accurate but is a fairly reliable sex characteristic, especially in the "wild" color pattern (the green budgies). In gray cockatiels, the males have a brighter yellow face patch and orange cheek patch than the females.

The First Veterinary Visit

Your bird should come with a health guarantee that requires a checkup by a veterinarian with a few days (usually 48 hours) after purchase. All pets including birds need regular veterinary examinations. Select a doctor knowledgeable about birds. Ask your vet for recommendations if he doesn't treat birds, or ask the person who sold you the bird for a recommendation. Otherwise, the local veterinary society can give you a referral. Most veterinarians who treat birds are members of the AAV (Association of

Avian Veterinarians) and regularly keep up with the latest continuing education on pet birds.

The first visit includes, at minimum, a thorough physical examination. Your vet will also recommend lab tests to determine the bird's health status. Unlike dogs and cats, but similar to other exotic pets discussed in this book, birds retain wild characteristics. One such characteristic is the "preservation response." This means that a bird will not act sick until it's dying and can't hide its illness anymore. In the wild, if a bird acted sick every time it felt bad, it would be quickly killed by its own flock members or predators. Therefore, birds can appear healthy yet be terminally ill. It is not uncommon for an owner to tell me that her pet bird, now discovered dead in its cage, was fine last night and was even eating and drinking! Due to this preservation response, *any* change in a bird's behavior (any deviation from what it normally does) is considered a serious and potentially life-threatening sign that must be investigated immediately by a veterinarian. A sick bird is a dying bird!

Laboratory testing will often reveal signs of illness in a bird that appears otherwise "healthy." For this reason, lab tests *must* be run on your new pet (and annually as well). Lab tests can include blood tests to check for infection, diabetes, and liver and kidney disease; gram stains of the choana (throat) and cloaca (common opening for the digestive, urinary, and reproductive systems) to check for abnormal yeasts and bacteria; radiographs (X-rays) to check for infection, tumors, or organ enlargement; cultures (if needed) to confirm a yeast or bacterial infection; and a test to check for psittacosis, a disease particularly common in budgies and cockatiels which is transmissible to people. Other tests can be done as recommended by your veterinarian. Often, these tests are done under a short anesthetic. Avian vets use isoflurane, an expensive but extremely safe gas anesthetic. Performing tests under anesthesia is often less stressful for the bird, owner, and hospital staff, and the risk is minimal. The most stressful thing someone can do to your bird is to restrain it; anesthesia is much less stressful and therefore safer for the bird.

At the first veterinary visit, we often trim the nails and beak, clip the wings, and remove the leg band. Leg bands serve no purpose on a pet bird. If not removed, they are a potential danger to the bird as a band can easily get caught in the cage, resulting in a fractured (broken) leg for the bird. Nails and beaks are trimmed whenever they get too long; how often trimming is needed depends upon your own bird, but at least quarterly should suffice for most pets. Wing feathers are clipped to decrease the chance of flying and are clipped whenever they are molted (usually quarterly). You need to be aware that even with clipped wings, some birds can still fly! Therefore, never take your bird outside (even for its trip to the doctor) unless it is safely contained in a cage or carrier!

I know that by now you're probably thinking that all of this is going to cost a lot of money. It's not unusual for owners of budgies and cockatiels to refuse all of these lab tests with the excuse that "the bird only cost $20." This is understandable; nevertheless, the lab tests are needed for *all* birds. If you don't give permission for the testing, your veterinarian can't possibly comment on your bird's health, and often the guarantee from the seller is void. The more information you can give your vet (by agreeing to the lab tests), the more he can tell you. Whenever someone with a sick bird refuses to spend money on the lab test, I tell them that I have no idea why their pet is sick and therefore have no idea how to treat it. The only thing I can do is guess what is wrong, and since so many things can cause a bird's illness, I have to treat for all of them. This means a bird may need to be on three or four medications that must be given several times a day! The moral is to spend the money on the tests and find out what's wrong, especially since some bird diseases are transmissible to people!

Housing

There is not a lot to say about how birds are housed other than they obviously live in cages. The best advice I can give is the cage, *at minimum*, obviously should allow the bird to stretch its wings the full length and to be able to turn around. Most owners of smaller birds have adequate size cages for their birds. I suppose it's possible to buy a cage that is too big, although other than wasting your money, there probably would be no harm to the bird. (It might be hard to catch the bird in a large cage if the bird is not hand-tame, and the bird could potentially injure itself flying away from an owner's hands in a large cage.)

Some comments need to be made about what goes in the cage, however. Cuttlebone, a mineral supplement, is safe to offer birds. Most of the time, the cuttlebone is placed in the cage and left there until it wears down, and then changed. Not all birds will use cuttlebone, however. No studies have shown that the cuttlebone is actually beneficial to birds, but it certainly won't cause any harm, and it may provide some calcium to the pet.

Grit, which is essentially small ground-up stone, used to be recommended by many avian (bird) veterinarians. It was felt that the grit helped the bird digest its food. We now know that grit is not necessary for birds. Birds have a muscular stomach called a gizzard which is very able to digest any type of food on its own. Grit has been found to harm and kill birds, however! Many birds, even sick ones, can engorge on grit and literally end up with a gizzard full of stones. This causes an impaction or blockage in the system. Often, only surgery will cure the problem. Birds suffering from grit impactions are usually seen in a very debilitated condition and are a poor surgical risk. Many owners may not want to subject their birds to surgery since there is a high risk, and many owners many not want to bear the cost of surgery on a small, inexpensive bird. A new technique used on larger birds that is often successful involves a flushing technique to aspirate the grit from the gizzard. Under anesthesia, a tube is passed into the gizzard. The water is then aspirated back through the syringe, removing the grit with it. Obviously, we'd rather prevent this condition by not offering bird grit in the first place.

Toys can be safely placed in a bird's cage as long as the smallest piece of the toy is too big to be swallowed by the bird. This means that toys for cockatiels shouldn't be offered to large parrots. Occasionally, a bird might swallow a small piece of the toy and develop an impaction (as with grit) or develop metal poisoning if the item was metallic. Birds like shiny things, such as jewelry, so care must be taken and jewelry not offered to birds.

Perches can cause problems for birds. Plastic perches and sandpaper perches are not recommended, as they predispose birds to foot problems, specifically an infection called bumblefoot. Wooden dowels or actual tree branches are recommended. If you want to use natural branches, here's a tip: When you get the branch from your tree, bake it in the oven for about 30 minutes at 350 degrees to kill any bugs that might be on it. The branches can be replaced as needed or washed when they get dirty, just like the wooden dowels.

Cages should be cleaned at least weekly with soap and water (rinse well). Line the cage with newspaper, which is inexpensive and easily replaced. Avoid litter, corncob bedding, and crushed walnut shells. These materials hold in moisture which can lead to bacterial growth. Also, some birds eat these bedding materials, which can lead to impactions or toxicity.

Diet

As with so many exotic pets, proper diet is critical for the well-being of pet birds. Contrary to what you've heard, an all seed diet is the *worst* thing for pet birds! Do not give your pet birdseed as its sole food source. Among avian (pet bird) veterinarians, we refer to an all-seed diet as a *death diet*!

This is because birds eating nothing but seeds will become afflicted with and die of diseases directly related to that diet at some point in their lives.

Seeds are very high in fat, which is why birds love them. However, seeds are very low in calcium and vitamins A, D, and E. A bird eating this nutritionally inadequate diet is prone to all sorts of troubles, especially secondary bacterial infections, hepatic lipidosis, and lipomas (see Diseases).

Many owners tell me their birds won't eat anything except seeds. Invariably, this is because seeds are left in the cage 24 hours a day. When a new food is introduced (such as vegetables or pellets), the bird either ignores the new item or throws it out of the cage. The only way to get a bird to eat something new is by offering the new item as the *only* food source and meal-feeding the bird (versus leaving seed available all day and night).

What should a bird eat? We recommend vegetables and fruit (about 80% veggies, 20% fruit) in the morning, with the cereal grains (mainly pellets) offered in the evening. Water can be left in the cage 24 hours a day as long as it's fresh (change the water at least twice daily to prevent bacteria and yeast growth). Water-soluble vitamins can be mixed in with each water change. I like Vivi 13+ by Lafeber.

Here is the schedule we recommend to bird owners trying to convert their seed-eating pets to a better diet. The idea is to gradually wean a bird onto a new, unfamiliar diet. Seeds are not offered in the morning, and therefore the bird will be hungry at the morning feeding and start playing with or nibbling on the vegetable mix.

1. Limit the amount of seeds. Feed the correct amount of seeds and one Avi-Cake at the evening feeding. (Avi-Cakes are a combination of seeds and pellets that are useful for switching a bird from seeds to a pelleted diet.) For any bird, but especially the smaller species, Avi-Cakes can be used by themselves as the grain source if the owner doesn't wish to go to an all-pellet diet at the

evening feeding. As a rule, feed one teaspoon of seed per 50-100 grams of body weight. Check with your veterinarian to see if his recommendations differ. (Incidentally, don't waste your money on vitamin-impregnated seeds. The vitamins are sprayed on the shells, which aren't eaten by the bird anyway.)

2. Remove any remaining food at bedtime. Water (without the Vivi-13+ vitamins mixed in) can be left in the cage or can be removed.

3. For the morning feeding, offer a variety of vegetables (80% of the offering) and fruits, cheeses, and eggs (20%). Variety is the key; the pieces should be cut into the appropriate size for the particular species of bird. Offer freshly prepared water and the vitamins.

4. In the evening, remove the veggie mix and replace it with the seeds and one Avi-Cake.

5. Once the bird shows interest in the Avi-Cakes, decrease the amount of seed so that the bird is eventually eating only Avi-Cakes (although seed can, at the owner's discretion, make up 10-20% of the evening meal).

6. If the bird loves the Avi-Cake on the first offering, you can immediately offer more Avi-Cakes at the next feeding and reduce or eliminate the seeds. On average, if Avi-Cakes are the only grain source offered at the evening feeding, offer 2-3 cakes per 100 grams of body weight.

7. Some birds take many weeks to begin accepting a new diet. If that is the case, decrease the amount of seed by 10% each week until the bird begins eating the Avi-Cakes. If you have decreased the seeds by 50% and the bird still shows no interest in the Avi-Cakes, contact your veterinarian for further advice (maybe your bird would like a different product, or maybe it's one of the few that will never eat anything except seeds).

8. Most birds will start eating the Avi-Cakes and the vegetables within a few weeks. Be patient!

This is the basic program used to convert seed-eating birds to a proper diet. Each veterinarian has his own method as well as favorite products to recommend. Once the bird is eating the veggies and Avi-Cakes, he can be weaned off of seeds entirely and eat just the Avi-Cakes. Often we will try weaning from the Avi-Cakes onto a pelleted diet using the program discussed above, gradually replacing Avi-Cakes with pellets.

Suitable vegetables and fruits to offer at the morning feeding include carrots, sweet potatoes, corn, kale, cabbage, spinach, green beans, green peas, various squashes, collard/turnip/mustard greens, alfalfa sprouts, apples, pears, peaches, strawberries, and bananas. Small pieces of cheese and cooked egg (hard-boiled or scrambled) can also be offered. Vegetables can be fresh (most desirable), frozen and thawed, or canned (least desirable). Fresh veggies can be offered raw (after thoroughly cleaning them) or cooked; each bird has its own preference. Spinach or cabbage, if offered, should be fed in small amounts. Notice that lettuce and celery are not listed, as they are low in nutrients. Avoid avocados (they are toxic). Candies, cookies, and chocolate should also be avoided.

For the evening meal, cooked pasta (rice, spaghetti, etc.) can be added to the grain (seeds, Avi-Cakes, pellets) mixture.

Common Diseases

As stated in the introduction, I am only mentioning the diseases I most commonly see in practice. Because most of you are first-time owners and probably own a budgie or cockatiel, I will concentrate on the diseases these two species most often acquire.

For most illnesses in birds, the best way to treat them is with injectable medications. This means that owners must be shown how to give their birds medications. Oral medications rarely work (a notable exception is the treatment for the disease psittacosis), and injections are actually easier for the bird and the owner than trying to force medicine into a bird's mouth. While the initial reaction of owner often is negative, most don't mind the injections once they are trained in giving the shots. Because most oral medications are ineffective, you should *never treat a bird with the oral antibiotics available at pet stores!* Many of the dying birds we attempt to save have been treated for several days with these oral medications. These medications only prevent pet owners from seeking early medical care!

Bacterial Infections

Bacterial infections are probably the most common infections I see in all species of birds. All of us live in a world of bacteria, yeasts, and viruses. Anytime we are stressed and our immune system isn't quite up to par, we are more prone to infections and disease. When we are not stressed and our immune systems are working properly, we are able to fight off most infections and not become ill. The same is true with birds. Birds are exposed to bacteria every day in the air, their food, their water, their toys, their cages, and their owners' mouths. (When you kiss your bird, you transmit microorganisms to your bird, and many vets advise against this common practice.) Animals and people have different types of bacteria normally located on them and in them that at any moment could cause disease. Therefore, it's hard to say exactly where most birds "pick up" an infection. What we can say is that birds in dirty cages (cages should be cleaned weekly, at least) and eating nothing but seeds (nutritionally inadequate; poor diet is a common stressor) are very likely to come down with an infection, and usually it's a bacterial infection. Seeds are low in many nutrients, but specifically vitamin A. Vitamin A is necessary for normal epithelium (skin and lining of body organs).

When there is not enough vitamin A in the diet, the epithelial linings of the body are more prone to infections with the microorganisms normally located on their surfaces. A bird on an all-seed diet is literally an accident waiting to happen, a bird waiting to die.

What kinds of infections are we talking about? Well, any part of the bird can become infected, but many sick birds are septic to some degree, which means their blood is infected and therefore the whole bird is also infected. The typical sick bird is not eating, is fluffed up and lethargic, and doesn't move much. While any disease can show these signs, these birds are definitely dying and many have at the very least a severe bacterial infection (some birds have other diseases as well!).

These infections can usually be easily diagnosed with gram stains, cultures, and blood tests. Treatment is begun before lab results are available and can be changed as these results are reported. The sicker birds are hospitalized and placed in an incubator. Since any stress, even handling them, can kill these birds, very little may be done until the bird becomes stabilized in the incubator. Often, antibiotic and vitamin injections and fluids are given without any lab tests being performed, as collecting lab samples might be too stressful and kill the bird. Sometimes, these sick birds are anesthetized just to treat them and collect samples; the anesthesia is often less stressful than handling the bird.

If the bird is showing mild symptoms that do not warrant hospitalization, it can be treated by the owner at home pending lab results. One or two different antibiotics are prescribed pending culture results.

Despite what many owners have heard, *with early diagnosis and treatment, most birds will recover*. This statement has several implications; diagnosis must be made *early* in the course of the disease. Since birds don't act sick until they've been sick for a while, a sick bird should be examined *at the first sign of illness!* Early diagnosis and treatment means you must spend money in order to properly diagnose and treat the illness.

For birds that are lying on the bottom of the cage in severe distress (near death), only about 25% or so will live despite diagnosis and treatment. However, since it's impossible to tell if your bird is one of these 25%, diagnosis and treatment should always be attempted.

Psittacosis

This disease, also called chlamydiosis or parrot fever, can occur in many birds but is especially common in budgies and cockatiels. Psittacosis is caused by a bacterial-type of organism called a chlamydia. The disease can actually take several forms: sudden death, a chronically sick bird (usually showing respiratory or gastrointestinal signs), or a healthy bird that carries the chlamydial organisms and sheds them in its droppings, infecting other birds and people. Since psittacosis can look like many diseases, any sick bird should be suspected of having it until laboratory testing proves otherwise. Likewise, since healthy birds can harbor the organism, all birds should be tested for this (we require a negative test before boarding birds).

Several types of tests are available; we use a blood test or a cloacal swab to diagnose the problem in the living bird. Tissue analysis can identify the organism in dead birds.

In budgies and cockatiels, the most common sign is a respiratory infection. Often birds have eye or nasal discharges. These signs are also seen with a mycoplasma infection. While treatment is similar for both diseases, it's important to differentiate between the two, as psittacosis is treated for a minimum of 45 days while mycoplasma is normally treated for about a week. Treatment involves oral tetracycline-type drugs; during treatment, an antifungal drug is also given, as yeast overgrowth is common in pets taking tetracycline medications.

In people, the disease causes flu-like symptoms. People who own birds and develop flu-like symptoms should contact their own physician about the possibility of psittacosis.

Candida

Candida is a yeast infection. While it can occur secondary to treatment for other diseases (especially if a tetracycline-type drug is used), it can occur as a primary infection as well. Common in cockatiels, it is usually seen as a crop infection, resulting in regurgitation. However, as with bacteria, candida can infect any organ in the body and cause sudden death. The crop infection is easily diagnosed with a crop washing and microscopic examination of the washing. Treatment is usually with oral nystatin, an antifungal drug.

Viral Diseases

Not as often diagnosed as other diseases, many viruses can plague birds, including herpes virus (which causes Pacheco's disease), papovavirus, pox virus, and the virus that causes Psittacine Beak and Feather disease (bird AIDS). For the most part, viral diseases don't have a specific treatment but require supportive care.

Cancer

Among birds, the budgerigar has the highest incidence of both benign and malignant tumors. The most common benign tumor is a fatty tumor called a lipoma; the most common malignant tumor affects the gonad (testicle or ovary) or kidney and usually results in a bird that is lame in one leg. (Most owners attribute this to a broken leg; in actuality it is the tumor putting pressure on the nerves supplying the leg.)

Some small tumors respond well to surgical removal; lipomas may shrink if a thyroid supplement is given and if the dietary fat is lowered. Other tumors may require chemotherapy, and yet others may not be treatable due to the location of the tumors (such as the gonad or kidney tumors mentioned above).

Obesity

This disease is common in both budgies and cockatiels due to an all-seed diet and occasionally, hypothyroidism (low thyroid) in the budgies. These birds are grossly overweight and may have actual fatty tumors. Death can occur suddenly from fatty liver disease (especially in cockatiels) or breathing difficulty from excess chest or abdominal fat. Obese birds are fragile, must be handled correctly, and must have their dietary fat content carefully lowered under veterinary supervision. Obese birds may also be prone to a stroke syndrome as well.

Hepatic Lipidosis

Also called "fatty liver disease," this condition is most commonly seen in obese birds fed an all-seed diet. Clinical signs are those seen with any illness and include loss of appetite, lethargy, and a ruffled appearance. Often the liver, which has become enlarged as fat accumulates, can be palpated (felt) during the physical examination. Radiographs (X-rays) also show the liver enlargement. Blood tests, while not diagnostic for this disease, do confirm a liver problem and any secondary illnesses as well. A liver biopsy is essential for accurate diagnosis, although with a good history and lab tests, a presumptive diagnosis can be made. Many of these birds are dying and require extensive hospitalization and treatment. As the bird improves, switching to a suitable diet is imperative. Some of these birds are so ill that even handling them can kill them.

Mange

External parasites are rare in most pet birds. Budgies commonly get something called scaly leg and face mites, or Knemidocoptic mange. Caused by a mite, a microscopic parasite, the condition is seen as scaly growths of the beak and/or feet. While the mites can be transmitted to cagemates, often only one bird in a group is infected. Many avian veterinarians feel that a genetic predisposition exists. Your vet will treat the condition with ivermectin and may recommend cleaning the cage. It is not transmissible to other pets or owners. The mite sprays and insecticide disks sold at pet stores are ineffective in preventing or treating this condition.

Internal Parasites

These are not as common as in dogs and cats but can occur. Often no gastrointestinal signs are seen, and the parasites are diagnosed during the annual exam on a fecal flotation test. In cockatiels, a protozoa called Giardia is often seen. Signs include violent feather picking and often the passing of whole seeds in the droppings. Treatment with an oral antiprotozoal medication usually alleviates the problem.

Diabetes Mellitus

Birds do get diabetes. The disease is usually easy to diagnose but difficult to treat. Current research indicates that unlike people, birds may not be insulin deficient, but may have another derangement of their glucose metabolism. Usually, birds with diabetes drink a lot and urinate frequently.

Fractures

All birds are prone to broken legs and wings. Removal of leg bands is the best preventative measure for broken legs. Fortunately, fractures heal well and quickly in most birds, especially the smaller ones.

Egg Problems

Many owners are surprised to learn that a solitary pet bird can lay eggs without a mate! Often these birds are thought to be males until one day an egg is seen in the cage. Any female bird can lay eggs with or without a mate. If no mate is present, of course the egg will not be fertile.

Two problems exist with egg-laying females. The first, often seen in cockatiels, is chronic egg laying. Egg production is stressful to a bird. Often these cockatiels are eating a diet composed of nothing but seeds, which are low in calcium. The egg production further lowers their calcium, as well as puts a nutritional stress on a bird that is eating a deficient diet. Any illness can result from this stress. Getting the hen to stop laying eggs can be a challenge. Behavioral therapy is tried first, with hormonal injections and an ovariohysterectomy used as a last resort.

Egg binding occurs when the egg is unable to be expelled from the female's body. The calcium-deficient diet is a common cause of this problem. Female birds that act sick in any way should be suspected of egg binding until proven otherwise. These birds are often on the bottom of the cage and may make straining attempts to lay the egg. Treatment is usually successful and includes placing the bird in the incubator, giving fluids, and often administering an injection of calcium or oxytocin (to stimulate uterine contractions). Occasionally, the doctor will need to aspirate the contents of the egg by passing a small needle through the bird's body and into the uterus. This is done in an attempt to collapse the empty egg shell in the hope that it will pass from the body. In rare cases surgery may be needed to remove the egg.

Lead Poisoning

Like ferrets, birds are curious creatures and are especially attracted to shiny objects. As stated previously, pieces of toys and jewelry are easily swallowed, and lead poisoning is suspected in any sick bird, especially if it's regurgitating or showing neurological signs. Radiographs (X-rays) of the bird often reveal the metal object, and blood tests can be used to check for lead and the anemia that often results from lead poisoning. Treatment for small lead particles involves injections of a drug that binds the lead in the bloodstream. Often surgery or intestinal flushing is needed with medicinal therapy to remove larger objects. Prevention is definitely preferred. Toys that are easily broken or dismantled should not be offered to birds. The toy should be appropriate for the species of bird: a parrot doesn't need a cockatiel toy that can be easily swallowed. Do not allow birds to play with jewelry.

Foot Necrosis/Gangrene

This condition is usually seen in the smaller birds such as finches and canaries. It results from the fine fiber or thread material sold so commonly in pet stores as "nesting material." The bird unravels the material and gets some of it caught around a toe, foot, or leg. This acts like a tourniquet (similar to wrapping a string around your own finger) and cuts off the blood supply. This condition is an emergency, as often the affected body part dies within a few hours once the blood supply has been cut off. On examination you will notice redness and swelling occurring early after the constriction. Within a few hours, the body part becomes purple, black, or blue.

When diagnosed early, treatment for this malady involves removing the thread material under anesthesia. Once the necrosis (death) occurs, amputation is the only treatment. Without it, gangrene will set in and the pet will die. Smaller birds do well even if the lower leg has to be amputated.

These are just some of the diseases we see on a regular basis. Certainly, birds are afflicted with more diseases, although they are not as common as the conditions mentioned in this chapter. Different diseases affect different species of birds; your veterinarian can review these with you.

Index

R

S

T

U

V

W

Y

Z

Other Books From Republic of Texas Press

Alamo Movies
by Frank Thompson

100 Days in Texas: The Alamo Letters
by Wallace O. Chariton

At Least 1836 Things You Ought to Know About Texas but Probably Don't
by Doris L. Miller

Classic Clint: The Laughs and Times of Clint Murchison, Jr.
by Dick Hitt

Country Savvy: Survival Tips for Farmers, Ranchers, and Cowboys
by Reed Blackmon

Critter Chronicles
by Jim Dunlap

Dallas Uncovered
by Larenda Lyles Roberts

Defense of a Legend: Crockett and the de la Peña Diary
by Bill Groneman

Dirty Dining: A Cookbook, and More, for Lovers
by Ginnie Siena Bivona

Don't Throw Feathers at Chickens: A Collection of Texas Political Humor
by Charles Herring, Jr. and Walter Richter

Exotic Pets: A Veterinary Guide for Owners
by Shawn Messonnier, D.V.M.

Exploring the Alamo Legends
by Wallace O. Chariton

From an Outhouse to the White House
by Wallace O. Chariton

The Funny Side of Texas
by Ellis Posey and John Johnson

The Great Texas Airship Mystery
by Wallace O. Chariton

Great Texas Golf: A Complete Directory to All Texas Golf Courses
by Pat Seelig

Just Passing Through
by Beth Beggs

Kingmakers
by John R. Knaggs

The Last Great Days of Radio
by Lynn Woolley

Other Books From Republic of Texas Press

Noble Brutes: Camels on the American Frontier
by Eva Jolene Boyd

Outlaws in Petticoats
by Ann Ruff and Gail Drago

Rainy Days in Texas Funbook
by Wallace O. Chariton

San Antonio Uncovered
by Mark Louis Rybczyk

Slitherin' 'Round Texas
by Jim Dunlap

Spirits of San Antonio and South Texas
by Docia Schultz Williams and Reneta Byrne

Texas Highway Humor
by Wallace O. Chariton

Texas Politics in My Rearview Mirror
by Waggoner Carr and Byron Varner

Texas Tales Your Teacher Never Told You
by Charles F. Eckhardt

Texas Wit and Wisdom
by Wallace O. Chariton

That Cat Won't Flush
by Wallace O. Chariton

That Old Overland Stagecoaching
by Eva Jolene Boyd

They Don't Have to Die
by Jim Dunlap

This Dog'll Hunt
by Wallace O. Chariton

To The Tyrants Never Yield
by Kevin R. Young

A Trail Rider's Guide to Texas
by Mary Elizabeth Sue Goldman

Unsolved Texas Mysteries
by Wallace O. Chariton

Western Horse Tales
Edited by Don Worcester